Handbook

on

Wood Preservation

Wood preservation is wood perpetuation.

THE PETERO PUB. & TG. CO., BALTO.

FOREWORD.

Wood properly preserved is practically permanent wood, and because efficient avoids the cost of unnecessary replacements. The treatment of timber to make it last the limit of its serviceability is a fundamental feature of modern engineering. Briefly, in the following pages, the American Wood-Preservers' Association presents facts and figures for those becoming interested in the subject. Further information will be cheerfully given by any of its members or officers (see pages 47-55). Reference to the literature listed on pages 56-73 also is recommended. The most comprehensive publications on the subject are the Proceedings of the American Wood-Preservers' Association and Howard F. Weiss' "Preservation of Structural Timber." For the guidance of treating-plant operators, construction engineers, and others interested in the technique of wood preservation, the American Wood-Preservers' Association will soon issue the beginnings of a Manual of Recommended Practice.

By up-to-date methods and in conformity with the best practice wood can be so preserved that its life is prolonged to at least three times what it would be without treatment. Consumers of wood can figure the savings for their own particular service, after getting quotations from their nearest wood-preserving plant. Large users of treated wood estimate savings as follows: Ties, 2 to 10 cents per tie per year; piles, 20 to 100 cents per pile per year; poles, 5 to 15 cents per pole, per year; posts, 1 to 3 cents per post per year; mine timbers, 2 to 3 dollars per gangway set per year.

CONTENTS.

CONTENTS

Wood Preservatives:

Manufacturers of or Dealers in Wood Preservatives:

Uses of Preserved Wood:

Manufacturers of Wood-Preserving Equipment:

Users of Preserved Wood:

Wood-Preserving Plants:

American Wood-Preservers' Association:

Bibliography of Wood Preservation:

HANDBOOK

ON

WOOD PRESERVATION.

DECAY, PREPARATION AND TREATMENT OF WOOD.

Recent research has shown that the decay of wood is due to the functions of low forms of plant life known as fungi, not to fermentation of sap or soil reaction. These fungi feed on certain substances in the wood and so dissolve the wood structure that it crumbles. Thus is produced punky or rotten wood. Evidence of the existence of a fungus is to be had in the form of a "bracket," "conk," "dog ear," "punk," "rabbit ear," "toadstool," etc., which projects from a surface of wood. These external growths are the fruiting bodies of the fungi and their functions are to produce spores, or seeds, which adhere to them until dislodged by the air or other disseminating mediums. Wherever these spores alight on wood and find conditions favorable, they germinate and develop into destructive agencies. In addition to spreading by means of spores or seeds, fungi extend themselves from one piece of wood to another by growing over small intervening spaces. Consequently decaying wood is a menace to all sound wood in the vicinity.

To develop, fungi require air, food, moisture and warmth. Dampness is the most favorable condition for them. Since the control of atmosphere, precipitation, and temperature are not practicable with wood used outdoors, the surest way to stop fungi is to poison their food supply by injecting into wood substances on which they cannot subsist.

The various woods available for use in the United States differ widely in their lasting quality, or ability to resist decay. While the sap portion of all woods will soon decay under exposure to the weather, the heartwoods of catalpa, cedar, chestnut, cypress, locust, some oaks, some pines, redwood, walnut, and a few other woods are durable.

The growing scarcity and high prices of woods which remain sound long dictates in many localities the use of woods not so durable. The greatest economy is to be effected by confining preservative treatment to woods which are not of themselves resistant to decay, because these often-otherwise-unserviceable woods are obtainable at comparatively-low cost. How helpful preservatives are in enlarging the number of usable woods may be seen in the following lists of kinds which without treatment could not render satisfactory service:

Posts		Ties	
Ash	Gum	Ash	Hickory
Basswood	Hickory	Beech	Maple
Beech	Maple	Birch	Oak (Red)
Birch	Oak (Red)	Elm	Pine (Sap)
Butternut	Pine (Sap)	Gum	Sycamore
Cottonwood	Poplar		
Elm	Sycamore		
	Willow		

The consumption of treatable woods as cross-ties is to be seen in the following figures for 1915:

Oaks, 16,885,517; southern pine, 8,541,203; Douglas fir, 3,553,854; western pine, 2,007,609; beech, 2,933,737; gum, 277,886; tamarack, 932,038; maple, 36,942; birch, 173,971; elm, 50,846; other species, 1,691,982; a total of 37,085,585 cross-ties.

The proper preparation of wood for treatment is essential to its successful preservation. Green wood resists the penetration of preservatives. The moisture which is in freshly fallen trees must be reduced in volume or consistency before it can be replaced by a preservative. This is accomplished by exposing the wood to the open air, by applying to it hot air in a kiln or steam in a closed cylinder, or by boiling it in hot oil. The method depends on the kind and the condition of the wood to be treated. But with any method for any kind of wood, the first step in its preparation for treatment is the removal of all bark.

Most woods can be prepared for treatment by being stacked on well-drained ground free from vegetation, in open piles for 4 to 12 months. In arid regions the piles should be less open than in humid regions, to avoid severe checking. Where wood splits while seasoning, irons of appropriate shape to stop the evil should be driven into the ends of the timber. Wood which is to dry in the open is preferably cut during winter, as spring and summer are the better seasoning periods.

The length of open-air preparation necessary or possible depends on the kind of wood, its dimensions, and the latitude of its storage. Oak may require 12 months seasoning in the vicinity of Philadelphia, while eight months may be enough around New Orleans. It might safely be held one and one-half times as long in either place. Gum, however, could and should be treated within eight months in the North and within four months in the South. The greater the surface area of a piece of wood in comparison to the volume, the more quickly will it dry. Most treated cross-ties are air-dried.

When open-air preparation is not feasible, steaming is usually resorted to. Care must be exercised that the pressure and its period are not carried to where the structure of the wood is injured. A vacuum is applied to dry the wood after its saturation by the steam. Most treated piles and structural timbers are prepared for treatment by steam.

On the Pacific Coast neither open-air nor steaming preparation is practiced. There the wood being treated is boiled in the creosote with which it is preserved.

After wood has been brought to a condition in which it can be treated it may be preserved by any of the processes referred to on pages 22-26.

The degree of treatment to be given varies with the kind and character of the wood and the service expected of it. In all cases the sapwood of treated material should be thoroughly penetrated by the preservative. The quantities of preservative usually left in timbers for various uses are as follows:

PRESERVATIVES INJECTED INTO WOOD.

Material Treated	Pounds Per Cubic Foot.	
	Creosote	Zinc Chloride
PILES:		
Salt Water	16 — 24	
Fresh Water	12 — 16	
Ground	8 — 12	
BLOCKS:		
Paving	16 — 20	
Flooring	6 — 12	¼ — ½
TIES	5 — 12	½ — ¾
TIMBER	8 — 16	¼ — ½

Since preservative treatment will not remedy structural defects of any kind, wood which is not free from decay or which has knots, splits, or other faults of sufficient size or number to weaken it for its purpose should not be treated.

Timber which has to be bored, dapped, mortised, or otherwise cut into during its erection should be so framed before treatment.

Preservation insures wood against deterioration.

CHRONICLE OF WOOD PRESERVATION.

The ancients were skilled in the art of preserving organic bodies. Pliny has said that they used garlic boiled in vinegar for protecting timber from attacks by worms. The early Egyptians embalmed their dead with oil of cedar, and later tar and linseed oil were recommended as preservatives. The Greeks and Romans recognized the antiseptic value of essential oils for preserving the wood they used in buildings. They also charred the wood to prevent decay. The Britons used to preserve the timbers of their warships against decay, either by soaking or coating them with petroleum oil, linseed oil, etc., and for a long time it was the practice to rub oil into the wood, or pour the oil into holes that had been bored into the wood. The Dutch early learned the advantage of preserving the timbers used in the construction of their dykes and marine structures by coating them with oil. The famous petroleum wells near Prome, in Burmah, furnished a good preservative for protecting wood used in ships and dwellings. But it was not until the early part of the nineteenth century that the preservation of wood by the injection of chemicals became scientific in principle and developed rapidly.

Numerous patents covering methods of preserving wood have been issued both in this country and abroad, and the early processes employing either animal oils, mineral oils or vegetable oils have been steadily improved. The mechanical operating features of these processes also have been improved, and the aim of the twentieth century wood-preserving plant is to afford wood as much protection against destruction as is possible, with as little preservative as will assure efficiency.

The growth of wood preservation in the United States from 1838, when the first cross-ties were treated by an infusion of bichloride of mercury and laid on the Northern Central Railroad in Maryland, now part of the Pennsylvania System, has been extraordinary.

The first commercial wood-preserving plant in the United States was built at Lowell, Mass., in 1848, using alternately bichloride of mercury and chloride of zinc, and it is still in operation.

The following chronological record of the wood-preserving industry begins in 1657, prior to which time authentic information is not available:

1657. Glauber experimented with vegetable pyroligneous acid (obtained by distillation of wood), first carbonizing the wood by fire, then covering it with tar and immersing the wood in the acid.

1705. Homberg used mercuric chloride for preserving wood.

1737. First American colonial privilege granted for preserving timber. Emerson patented a process for saturating timber with boiled oil mixed with poisonous substances.

1740. Reid proposed a method of using a vegetable acid (probably pyroligneous acid) as a bath for wood to protect it against decay.

1756. Hales recommended use of linseed oil for soaking planks at the water-line of ships to prevent decay.

1767. De Boissieu used mercuric chloride as a preservative. He and Bordenave recommended copper sulphate, the process being known as "Margaryizing."

1798. Volmeister washed and immersed wood in a solution of sea water.

1806. Perkins filled the interstices of wood with dry salt.

1809. First French patents on timber preservation granted as a result of the patent law created by Napoleon I.

1811. Lukin treated wood by burying it in pulverized charcoal in a heated oven.

1815. Wade recommended zinc chloride. Finding that alum was not a good preservative and rapidly decayed timber he suggested impregnation with resinous or oleaginous substances (especially linseed oil), or with common resin dissolved in a tank of caustic alkali, and subsequently plunged the wood into water acidulated with any cheap acid or with alum in solution. / Bowden immersed wood in sea water. Boydon, of the British Navy Office, advocated boiling in lime water timber blocks and tree nails of ships, followed by boiling in a thin solution of glue, by means of which the pores of the wood would be filled by a hard substance insoluble in water. Boydon also thought that glue might be used with lime water, or glue and lime water mixed together, to check the growth of vegetation and strengthen wood.

1817. Chapman used copper sulphate, and experimented with lime, soap and alkaline salts.

1820. Pasley first boiled wood in water, and applied acids and other concentrated liquids.

1821. Knowles and Davy immersed wood in mercuric chloride.

1822. Prechtl exposed wood to the vapor of water alone and then to a mixture of water and tar.

1823. Oxford coated wood with oil of tar, previously treated with gaseous chlorine.

1824. Cox saturated wood with a mixture of fish oil, rosin and sulphur.

1825. Langton extracted by a vacuum the air from heated wood.

1826. Newmarch boiled wood in a mixture of linseed oil, iron sulphate, verdigris, arsenic and alum.

1828. Gossier alternately immersed wood in saline solutions containing calcium chloride, Glauber salts, iron sulphate and sodium arsenate.

1829. Carey first perforated wood and then introduced a mixture of salt, powdered charcoal and animal or vegetable oil.

1831. Breant invented an apparatus for forcing preservative liquids into wood.

1832. Kyan patented the injection into wood by pressure in a closed cylinder of mercuric chloride. Oxford patented the coating of timber with lead oxide, calcium carbonate and carbon of purified coal-tar, ground and mixed with oil. In this year was also tried smoking green wood to create a protective coating against decay.

1833. Attempts to arrest decay in wood by immersing or coating it with tar and tobacco leaves; also coating with rosin dissolved in fish oil, and coating with india rubber dissolved in fatty oils.

1834. Strutzke and the Society of Arts of London introduced the method of repeatedly coating wood with a solution of iron sulphate.

1835. Monteith immersed wood in lime water. Concentrated sulphuric acid as a coating to carbonize wood was also tried by an investigator. First wood pavements for city streets in the United States were laid in New York.

1836. Moll patented process for treating wood with coal-tar creosote in a closed iron vessel. Chevalier coated wood with a solution of tar and tobacco leaves.

1837. Boucherie recommended the use of zinc chloride. Margary's patent granted for using copper sulphate. Flockton saturated wood with oil of tar and iron acetate. Letellier immersed wood in a solution of mercuric chloride, and when dry subjected it to a coat of glue. Granville used the refuse water of salt works to preserve wood. Gottheil immersed wood in resinous solutions containing tar, oil of turpentine, and salt. The Industrial Society of Annaberg, Germany, introduced the method of immersing wood for a month in soluble glass, then placing it in water acidulated with hydrochloride acid, washing and drying, and finally rubbing it with oil.

1838. Bethell patented process for using coal-tar creosote, injected into wood under pressure in a cylinder. This process is still in use. Burnett patented the use of zinc chloride. Chestnut cross-ties, treated by the Kyan process, laid on the Northern Central Railroad of Maryland.

1839. Boucherie patented the absorption by the tree while alive or immediately after cutting, of iron acetate, acetic acid, muriate of lime, copper sulphate, mercuric chloride and other chemicals. Kyanized hemlock cross-ties laid at the fortifications at Fort Ontario, New York.

1840. Feiselli, after steaming the wood, injected a solution of alum and potash, or soluble glass and dilute sulphuric acid. Munzing immersed wood in a solution of muriate or protoxide of manganese, the refuse liquid of chlorine works. Pine stringers, subjected to a lime bath, laid on Philadelphia & Columbia Railroad. Kyanized oak ties laid on the Chesapeake & Ohio Railroad, and bridge timber treated by the same process used at Alexandria, Va.

1841. Payne patented the treatment of wood first with a solution of muriate of lime, iron sulphate and potash, and then with alum and potash. Pons immersed wood in a solution of iron nitrate, saltpeter, alum, and potassium ferrocyanide.

1842. Timperly used mercuric chloride. Kyanized ties laid on Baltimore & Ohio Railroad.

1843. Parkes treated wood with caoutchouc dissolved in carburet of sulphur eupion. Earle immersed wood in a solution of iron sulphate or copper sulphate.

1844. Burkes first steamed the wood and then impregnated it with a solution of soluble glass and iron sulphate.

1845. Ransome, after removing the air from the wood, injected by pressure a solution of soluble glass, and later placed it in a diluted acid.

1846. The Eastern Massachusetts Railroad used the Kyan process. Blythe invented "thermo-carbolization," which consists in treating wood with carburetted steam to extract the sap and water, and at the same time inject into the wood creosote held in suspension. Payne, after extracting the air from wood, injected a solution of metallic sulphurets (lime and baryta), and finally an acid or metallic salt (iron sulphate, etc.). Venzat and Banner impregnated wood with a solution of sulphate or muriate of copper, and followed this with baryta.

1848. Wood preservation on a commercial scale began in the United States through building of a Kyanizing plant at Lowell, Mass., to treat timbers used in locks and canals on the Merrimac River. This plant is still in operation.

1849. New York Central Railroad used Kyanized cross-ties.

1850. Kyanized pine bridge timber used by the Philadelphia & Reading Railroad. First Burnettizing plant in America built at Lowell, Mass., to treat canal timbers.

1852. Philadelphia & Reading Railroad treated ties with tar.

1853. Fitchburg Railroad used Kyanized shop floor joists.

1854. Kyanized pine used for the Blackstone bridge of the New York & New England Railroad. Creosoted ties laid on Philadelphia & Reading Railroad.

1855. Burnettized spruce stringers and ties laid on the Union (horse) Railroad of Cambridge, Mass.

1856. Vermont Central Railroad erected a Burnettizing plant for treating hemlock cross-ties and bridge timbers.

1857. Burnettized spruce used by the Middlesex & South Boston Railroad, and on the Boston, Mass., wharf.

1860. Chicago, Rock Island & Pacific Railroad treated bridge timber with zinc chloride. Burnettized spruce bridge ties used on the Boston & Albany Railroad in Boston, Mass.

1861. Erie Railroad built a Burnettizing plant at Oswego, New York, which was burned in 1869, and has not been rebuilt.

1862. Burnettized bridge timber used by the Ohio & Mississippi Railroad.

1863. Philadelphia, Wilmington & Baltimore Railroad built Burnettizing plants, at Wilmington, Delaware, and Perryville, Maryland, to preserve timbers used in wooden bridge at Havre de Grace, Md.

1865. Old Colony Railroad erected a Bethell plant at Somerset, Mass., which is believed to be the first practical use of this process in the United States. Foreman applied to wood a dry powder of salt, arsenic and corrosive sublimate. Isaac Hinckley, late President of the Philadelphia, Wilmington & Baltimore Railroad, used creosote to preserve piles for bridge over the Taunton River on Old Colony Railroad in Massachusetts.

1866. Chicago, Rock Island and Pacific Railroad laid 2,000 Burnettized cross-ties.

1867. Philadelphia & Reading Railroad built a Burnettizing plant at Pottstown, Pa. So did the Union Pacific Railroad, at Omaha, Nebraska. Introduction of Robbins' process for smoking wood with the vapors of coal-tar and of creosote. Seeley patented pressure process for treating green timber with oleaginous and saline materials, and erected plants in New York, Chicago, and at the St. Clair Flats in Michigan, the United States Government using the process at the latter place for preserving the timbers along its canal. Burnettized ties used on the Lehigh & Susquehanna Railroad. W. H. Smith encased timber in vitrified earthenware pipes, and filled in with hydraulic cement.

1868. Seeley patented an open-tank process for treating green timber with creosote oil. Beer washed out the sap from wood with a solution of boiling borax.

1869. Louisville & Nashville Railroad treated stringers and piles with the Bethell Process.

1870. Thilmany used sulphate of copper or sulphate of zinc and chloride of barium in treating ties for the Baltimore & Ohio, Wabash, New York, Pennsylvania & Ohio, Lake Shore & Michigan Southern, Cleveland & Pittsburgh and other railroads.

1871. Thomas immersed wood in rosin oil. Webb bored holes in the wood and filled them with creosote.

1872. Fletcher boiled in coal-tar creosote some cypress paving blocks which were laid in New Orleans, La.] Constant and Smith tried to preserve wood by smoking it with vapors of coal-tar in a retort. Detwiler and Van Gilder impregnated wood with rosin dissolved in naphtha under pressure.

1874. Rutgers introduced in Germany a method of treating ties with a mixture of zinc chloride and creosote.

1875. Louisville & Nashville Railroad built a Bethell plant at West Pascagoula, La., to treat piles, stringers and ties. This plant laid the foundation for modern timber-treating in this country.

1876. Houston & Texas Central Railroad built a Bethell plant at Houston, Texas, to treat piles and timbers. Central Railroad of New Jersey installed cross-ties treated by the Bethell process.

1878. Commercial creosoting plant opened at Long Island City, New York.

1879. Boulton patented a process to extract the moisture from wood and simultaneously inject creosote. New Orleans & North Eastern Railroad built a pressure plant to treat with creosote, at Slidell, La., the timber to be used for a trestle across Lake Ponchartrain. Wellhouse employed zinc chloride, glue and tannin for preserving wood. Commercial creosoting plant built at Slidell, La.

1880. Houston & Tennessee Central Railway installed ties treated by the Bethell process. Pine piles treated by the Thilmany process used at Norfolk, Va.

1881. Commercial creosoting plant erected at Portsmouth, Va.

1882. Fladd patented process of impregnating freshly-cut wood with copper sulphate and other chemicals by suction.

1883. Hagen used gypsum as a plug for zinc-chloride treated wood.

1884. Boston & Maine Railroad installed Kyanized ties. Commercial creosoting plant erected at Seattle, Wash. Vulcanized pine ties laid on the Manhattan Elevated Railroad in New York City.

1885. Atchison, Topeka & Santa Fe Railroad built a Burnettizing plant at Los Vegas, New Mexico.

1886. Chicago, Rock Island & Pacific and the Union Pacific railroads used ties treated by the Wellhouse process. Lehigh Valley Railroad installed ties treated by the Bethell process.

1887. Southern Pacific Railway (Atlantic System) began treating Texas pine ties by the Burnett process at a leased plant.

1888. New Orleans Wood-Preserving Company erected a plant at New Orleans, La., to treat ties by the Burnett process, and piles and lumber by creosoting, for Texas & New Orleans Railroad.

1889. Southern Pacific Railway built a plant at West Oakland, Cal., employing either the Bethell or Curtis & Isaacs creosoting processes for treating ties and piles.

1890. Texas & New Orleans Railroad built a Bethell plant at Houston, Texas.

1891. Southern Pacific Railway (Atlantic System) built a Burnettizing plant at Houston, Texas. The D. & I. Railroad used ties treated by the Wellhouse process.

1892. Commercial Burnettizing plant built at Beaumont, Texas, and a commercial Bethell plant erected at the same place.

1893. Southern Pacific Railway (Pacific System) erected a portable Burnettizing plant for treating ties at Latham, Oregon.

1895. Louisville & Nashville Railroad put up a treating plant at Gautier, Miss., which was rebuilt in 1916. Commercial creosoting plants were built at Bay City, Mich., and Lowell, Wash.

1896. Pennsylvania Lines West installed ties treated by the Wellhouse process. Commercial creosoting plant was erected at Buell near Norfolk, Va.

1897. Atchison, Topeka & Santa Fe Railway built Burnettizing plants at Somerville, Tex., and at Bellemont, Arizona. Hasselman patented process for injecting into wood a solution of iron and aluminum sulphate, adding kainit to neutralize the free acids formed.

1899. Chicago, Burlington & Quincy Railroad erected a Burnettizing plant for treating ties at Sheridan, Wyoming. Chicago & Eastern Illinois Railroad used the Wellhouse process for treating ties. Commercial plant using the Burnettizing and Allardyce processes erected at Mt. Vernon, Illinois. Commercial plant vulcanizing ties removed from New York City to Perth Amboy, N. J., later using the creo-resinate process, and in 1906 transferred to Norfolk, Va.

1900. Chicago & Alton Railroad used Burnettized and creosoted ties and timbers.

1901. Great Northern Railway built a plant at Somers, Mont., to treat ties by Burnettizing. Missouri, Kansas & Texas Railroad used the Wellhouse process for treating ties at Greenville, Texas. Mexican Central Railway built a Burnettizing plant at Aguas Calientas, Mexico, to treat ties. Commercial creosoting plant erected at Southport near New Orleans, La., and one at Norfolk, Va. A non-pressure wood-preserving plant erected at Portland, Oregon. Bevier invented creo-resinate process.

1902. Rueping patented the injection of compressed air into wood ahead of creosote. El Paso & Southwestern Railroad erected a creosoting plant at Alamogorda, N. M., for treating paving blocks, wooden pipe and crossing plank. Chicago, Burlington & Quincy Railroad tried the Hasselman process. Commercial plants using various processes erected at Carbondale, Ill., and at Texarkana, Arkansas.

1903. Union Pacific Railroad erected a Burnettizing plant at Laramie, Wyo., for treating ties, telegraph poles, dimension timbers and crossing plank. Chicago & Northwestern Railway built a plant at Escanaba, Mich., for treating ties, using first the Wellhouse, then the Card and now the Burnett processes. Grand Trunk and Wabash Railroads installed Burnettized cross-ties. Commercial creosoting plant erected at Indianapolis, Ind., and one for using various processes built at Cimarron, N. M. Guissani open-tank process promoted in New York.

1904. Von Schrenk revived the Seeley open-tank process at the Exposition in St. Louis, Mo. Rueping took out United States patents. Oregon-Washington Railroad & Navigation Company erected a creosoting plant at Wyeth, Oregon, for treating ties, piles, switch-ties, dimension timbers, and paving blocks. Chicago, Milwaukee & St. Paul Railroad employed the Rueping process. The Big Four (Cleveland, Cincinnati, Chicago & St. Louis Railroad) used ties treated with creosote by a commercial wood-preserving plant at Shirley, Indiana. Kansas City Southern Railroad installed Burnettized cross-ties. Commercial plants for treating wood by various processes were erected at Grenada, Miss., Sandstone, Minn., and Terre Haute, Indiana. Organization of the Wood-Preservers' Association (changed to American Wood-Preservers' Association in 1912).

1905. Lowry patented pressure process, using creosote with quick final vacuum. The first plant to use the Lowry process was erected at Shirley, Indiana. St. Louis & Southwestern Railroad used zinc-creosote treated ties, and the T., St. L. & W. Railroad Burnettized cross-ties. Delaware, Lackawanna & Western Railroad installed creosoted bridge-ties. Salt Lake & San Francisco Railroad installed ties treated by the Rueping process. Commercial plant using Bethell process erected at Maurer, N. J. Other commercial creosoting plants were built at Galveston, Tex., and Minneapolis, Minn.

1906. Card invented an improvement on the zinc chloride-creosote process. Atchison, Topeka & Santa Fe Railway erected a creosoting plant at Somerville, Tex. Kansas City Southern Railroad used creosoted cross-ties. Commercial creosoting plants were erected at Gulfport, Miss., Winnfield, La., Eagle Harbor, Wash., and Newark, N. J., and a plant employing the Card process was built at Waukegan, Illinois.

1907. Northern Pacific Railway erected Lowry plants at Brainerd, Minn., and at Paradise, Montana. Florida East Coast Railroad installed creosoted cross-ties. Lowry plants were erected at Marion, Ill., Bloomington, Ind., Springfield, Mo., Kansas City, Mo., and Hugo, Oklahoma. Atchison, Topeka & Santa Fe Railway built a crude oil plant at Albuquerque, N. M., which was later used for creosoting. Commercial plants using various processes were erected at Argenta, Ark., Evansville, Ind., and Buell, Va. A commercial creosoting plant was built at Mobile, Alabama. The Chicago, Burlington & Quincy Railroad erected a plant at Galesburg, Ill., for treating ties and timbers with either creosote, or zinc chloride, or both in combination. Delaware, Lackawanna & Western Railroad built a non-pressure plant at Nanticoke, Pa., and the Philadelphia & Reading Coal and Iron Company a similar one at New Philadelphia, Pa. The United States Government operated non-pressure plants at Keokuk, Iowa, Milan, Ill., Stillwater, Minn., and Fountain City, Wis.

1908. San Pedro, Los Angeles & Salt Lake Railroad erected a plant at San Pedro, Cal., to use either the Burnett or creosoting processes.

Bunker Hill & Sullivan Mining Company built a creosoting plant at Kellogg, Idaho. A commercial Bethell plant was erected at Atlanta, Georgia. A Lowry process plant was put in operation at Brainerd, Minn., by the Northern Pacific Railway.

1909. Tennessee Coal, Iron and Railroad Company built a non-pressure creosoting plant at McAdory, Alabama, for treating ties, telegraph poles, dimension timbers, and fence posts. Missouri, Kansas & Texas Railway built a Rueping plant at Dennison, Tex., for treating practically all kinds of timber. Union Pacific Railway built a Burnett-izing plant at Topeka, Kansas. Pennsylvania Railroad erected a wood-preserving plant at Mt. Union, Pa. Commercial creosoting plants were erected at Bound Brook, N. J., Toledo, O., Paterson, N. J., and Columbus, Ohio. A commercial Burnettizing plant was built at Joppa, Ill., and a plant using various processes at Madison, Illinois.

1910. Pennsylvania Railroad erected a wood-preserving plant at Greenwich Point, Philadelphia, Pa. The Buffalo, Rochester & Pittsburgh Railroad built a Bethell plant at Bradford, Pa. Commercial creosoting plants erected at Shreveport, La., Rome, N. Y., Toledo, O., and Texarkana, Texas.

1911. A commercial creosoting plant erected at Ensley, Ala., and a plant for treating wood by various processes was built at Broadford Junction, Pa. The Pittsburgh & Lake Erie Railroad used creosoted ties.

1912. Philadelphia & Reading and Central Railroad of New Jersey erected a creosoting plant at Port Reading, N .J. Baltimore & Ohio Railroad built a Card process plant at Green Spring, W. Va. Atlantic Coast Line Railroad erected a Bethell plant at Gainesville, Florida. Central of Georgia Railroad put up a plant at Macon, Ga., to treat wood by the Card process. Charlotte Harbor & Northern Railroad built a creosoting plant at Hull, Florida. Commercial plants using various processes built at Terre Haute, Ind., Houston, Tex., Orrville, O., St. Helens, Oregon, Tacoma, Wash., Yardley, Wash., Pensacola, Fla., Louisville, Miss., Bogalusa, La., and Linnton near Portland, Oregon. Incorporation of the American Wood-Preservers' Association (formerly called Wood-Preservers' Association.)

1913. Louisville & Nashville Railroad erected a plant at Guthrie, Kentucky. Commercial creosoting plants built at Bay City, Mich., Metropolis, Ill., and Indianapolis, Ind.

1915. Chicago & Northwestern Railway erected a plant at Riverton. Wyo. Ties of the Chesapeake & Ohio, the Chesapeake & Ohio Northern and the Hocking Valley Railroads treated at a commercial Lowry plant at Russell, Ky. A commercial plant erected at Brunswick, Georgia.

1916. Boston Elevated Railway erected a creosoting plant at South Boston, Mass. A commercial creosoting plant built at Seattle, Wash.

PROGRESS IN WOOD PRESERVATION.

The growth of the wood-preserving industry in the United States, begun in an experimental way in 1832, has been rapid. At first Kyan's process of treating wood with bichloride of mercury was used, but real progress in wood preservation in this country did not begin until about 1838, when Burnett's zinc-chloride process and Bethell's coal-tar-creosote process for protecting wood against decay were introduced. Many other processes for preserving wood have been tried on a commercial scale with varying success, and manufacturers of machinery and supplies have made improvements that have made possible more economical operation of timber-treating plants. The merits of treated wood, notably its durability and economy in service, are also better known, and consumption is on the increase.

Undoubtedly the greatest impetus given to the wood-preserving industry in this country has been the advancing cost of timber, due to its wasteful consumption and increasing scarcity. At first the demand for treated wood was confined to comparatively few forms and kinds of material, because there was a large supply of cheap and durable timbers to be had, and as the equipment of the treating plant was expensive and the success of the processes considered uncertain, the early growth of wood preservation was slow.

Only 15 plants were in operation in the United States in 1895, but since then the number has rapidly increased. In 1914 there were 122 plants, of which 94 were in operation and reported an output of 159,582,639 cubic feet of treated timber, comprising railroad ties, piles, poles, paving blocks, structural timbers, cross-arms, lumber and miscellaneous kinds of wood. In 1915 the United States had no less than 127 plants of all kinds, and of these 102 were active, reporting a total output of 141,858,963 cubic feet of treated material. The accompanying table and diagrams will give some idea of the growth in output of treated timber in the United States from 1909 to 1915 inclusive.

The majority of the wood-preserving plants in the United States are of the pressure type; that is, the preservative solution is forced into the wood by means of pumps. Sixty-four of the plants in operation in 1915 were so-called commercial plants, which treat wood by contract, 30 were operated by railroads, and eight were owned by mining companies and municipalities. The location of these plants is shown on the map on page 21.

In 1915 the quantity of miscellaneous lumber treated in the Atlantic Coast Region exceeded that of any other region. There were treated in that year: 7,428,938 cross-ties; 3,500,821 linear feet of piles; 11,697 poles; 552,095 square yards of paving blocks; 28,298,805 board feet of construction timber; 16,757 cross-arms; 4,634,655 board feet of miscellaneous lumber. The preservatives used in this region in 1915 were: Creosote, 30,236,615 gallons; zinc-chloride, 2,077,877 pounds; other preservatives, 50,080 gallons. During the year 1915 there were 20 plants in operation in this region.

In the Southern Coast Region, the 27 plants in operation during 1915 held the lead in the quantity of construction timber treated. The output for that year was: Construction timber, 77,798,523 board feet; cross-ties, 8,958,293; piles, 3,817,927 linear feet; poles, 66,216; paving blocks, 806,968 square yards; cross-arms, 121,945; miscellaneous lumber, 3,658,227 board feet. Of creosote there was used during the year 25,854,013 gallons, and of zinc-chloride, 9,767,867 pounds.

PROGRESS OF WOOD PRESERVATION IN THE UNITED STATES
QUANTITIES OF MATERIAL TREATED BY WOOD PRESERVING PLANTS
1908–1915.

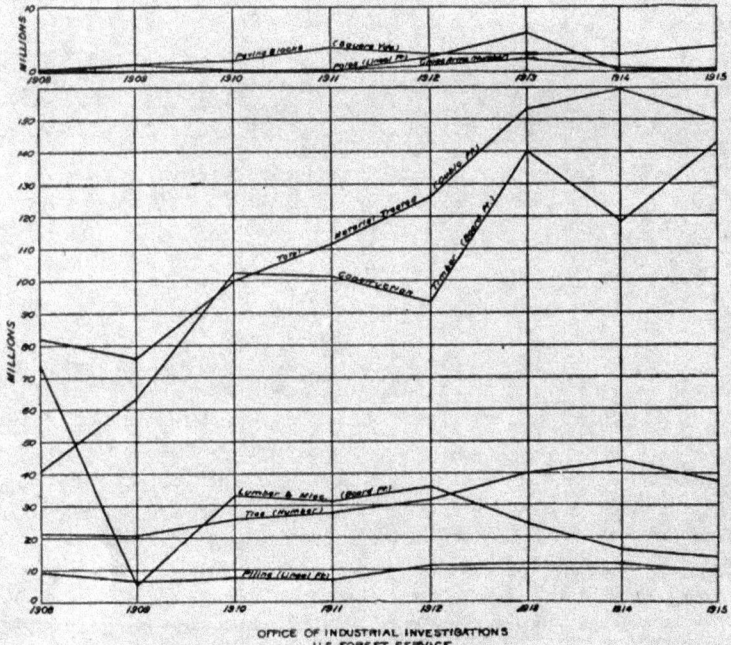

OFFICE OF INDUSTRIAL INVESTIGATIONS
U.S. FOREST SERVICE

The Interior Eastern Region led in the quantity of paving material handled, and showed the largest consumption of miscellaneous preservatives. The output of the 29 plants reporting in 1915 was: 14,650,302 cross-ties; 138,639 linear feet of piles; 32,503 poles; 1,509,755 square yards of paving blocks; 18,914,931 board feet of construction timber; 2,211 cross-arms; and 1,809,064 board feet of miscellaneous lumber. Of preservatives there were used 22,333,674 gallons of creosote, 12,764,-798 pounds of zinc-chloride, and 1,640,102 gallons other preservatives.

In the Interior Western Region, where 10 plants were in operation in 1915, the output was as follows: Cross-ties, 4,001,878; piles, 3,010 linear feet; poles, 3,107; paving blocks, 1,000 square yards; construction timber, 6,628,575 board feet; cross-arms, 56; miscellaneous lumber, 3,398,959 board feet. Of creosote there was used in 1915 a total of 2,395,411 gallons, and of zinc-chloride, 6,441,138 pounds.

The Pacific Coast Region had 16 plants in operation which reported the following output during 1915: Cross-ties, 2,046,177; piles, 1,848,022 linear feet; poles, 12,116; paving blocks, 66,552 square yards; construction timber, 10,368,207 board feet; cross-arms, 5,250; miscellaneous lumber, 436,604 board feet. The preservatives used in treating this timber were: Creosote, 3,245,292 gallons; zinc-chloride, 2,217,924 pounds; other preservatives, 3,362 gallons.

The output of the 102 plants in operation in the United States during 1915 was as follows:

Cross-ties	37,085,585 pieces.
Piles	9,308,419 linear feet.
Poles	125,939 pieces.
Paving Blocks	2,936,370 square yards.
Construction Timber	142,009,041 board feet.
Cross-arms	146,219 pieces.
Miscellaneous Lumber	13,937,509 board feet.

Total equivalent to..141,858,963 cubic feet.

The preservatives consumed in 1915 were as below:

Creosote (Foreign)	37,501,007 gallons.
" (Domestic)	43,358,435 "
Total	80,859,442 "
Zinc-chloride	33,269,604 pounds.
Other Preservatives	1,693,544 gallons.

In view of the fact that the railroads are the largest users of preserved wood, it is of interest to see the kinds of cross-ties that made up the 37,085,585 treated in 1915, and also the preservative used for each kind of wood, as given in the table on page 19.

The influence of railway practice on the growth of the wood-preserving industry is illustrated in the following table, which shows that the increase in the number of plants operated has been coincident with the increase in the number of ties treated.

Preserve wood and conserve woodland.

MATERIAL TREATED IN THE UNITED STATES.

Preservatives.	Year.	Cross Ties. Cu. Ft.	Piles. Cu. Ft.	Poles. Cu. Ft.	Paving Blocks. Cu. Ft.	Construction Timbers. Cu. Ft.	Cross-Arms. Cu. Ft.	Lumber and Miscellaneous. Cu. Ft.	Total Material Treated. Cu. Ft.
Creosote	1909	29,830,080	4,421,726	659,664	2,994,290	4,902,311	41,764	417,787	43,267,622
	1910	44,525,229	5,219,254	255,597	4,692,453	7,801,272	88,069	2,687,713	65,269,587
	1911	49,532,163	4,937,363	106,213	10,145,724	7,417,105	71,961	2,499,995	74,710,524
	1912	57,461,515	7,624,939	1,169,981	7,091,658	6,892,493	1,643,128	2,841,195	84,724,909
	1913	75,998,307	7,630,328	2,367,769	6,810,308	10,308,883	1,813,010	1,853,993	106,782,598
	1914	67,774,329	7,804,657	1,188,511	3,127,506	8,389,158	395,403	1,348,566	90,027,630
	1915	51,231,207	6,288,238	2,336,318	1,174,319	9,264,164	87,373	981,028	85,115,647
Zinc Chloride	1909	24,153,162	a	a	a	320,891	a	2,333	24,476,386
	1910	27,587,583	a	a	a	541,514	a	71,060	28,200,157
	1911	28,337,883	a	18,246	a	1,043,851	a	119,931	29,501,665
	1912	28,532,874	a	47,996	a	259,972	a	20,092	28,831,184
	1913	36,051,816	a	b	a	585,756	a	7,670	36,693,238
	1914	50,020,755	a	a	a	1,317,925	a	4,355	51,343,035
	1915	53,457,552	4,726	a	a	2,406,150	a	275,279	56,144,007
Zinc-Creosote	1909	8,095,794	a	a	a	62,918	a	43,699	8,202,411
	1910	6,354,219	38,392	a	a	181,143	a	30,646	6,604,400
	1911	7,312,374	b	a	a	b	a	b	7,312,374
	1912	8,214,303	97,874	a	b	560,613	a	99,367	8,972,157
	1913	6,938,838	327,594	a	b	758,989	a	53,628	8,079,049
	1914	5,868,834	a	a	b	140,718	a	b	6,009,552
	1915	6,548,136	2,320	110,220	a	40,396	a	4,822	6,705,894
All Preservatives	1909	62,079,036	4,421,726	659,664	2,994,290	5,286,120	41,764	463,819	75,946,419
	1910	78,467,031	5,257,646	255,597	4,692,453	8,523,929	88,069	2,789,419	100,074,144
	1911	85,182,420	4,937,363	106,213	10,145,724	8,460,956	71,961	2,619,926	111,524,563
	1912	97,183,009	7,737,035	1,188,579	7,397,095	7,793,524	1,643,128	2,988,686	125,931,056
	1913	120,781,248	7,957,922	2,500,420	6,856,293	11,653,628	1,824,719	2,039,658	133,613,888
	1914	131,540,961	8,061,902	1,482,407	6,869,370	9,847,801	417,914	1,362,284	159,582,639
	1915	111,256,755	6,295,284	2,512,780	7,707,971	11,834,087	90,627	1,161,459	141,858,963

NOTE.—Figures furnished by United States Forest Service. (a). No Statistics. (b). Figures, if used, would reveal identity of reporting firms.

CONVERTING FACTORS.

To obtain the number of cross ties, divide figures shown by 3.
To obtain the number of linear feet of piles, divide the figures shown by .6763.
To obtain the number of linear feet of poles, divide the figures shown by .5868.
To obtain the number of square yards of paving blocks, divide the figures shown by 2.625.
To obtain the number of board feet of construction timbers, multiply the figures shown by 12.
To obtain the number of cross-arms, divide the figures shown by .6198.
To obtain the number of board feet of lumber and miscellaneous material, multiply the figures shown by 12,

MATERIAL TREATED IN THE UNITED STATES.
TOTAL MATERIAL.

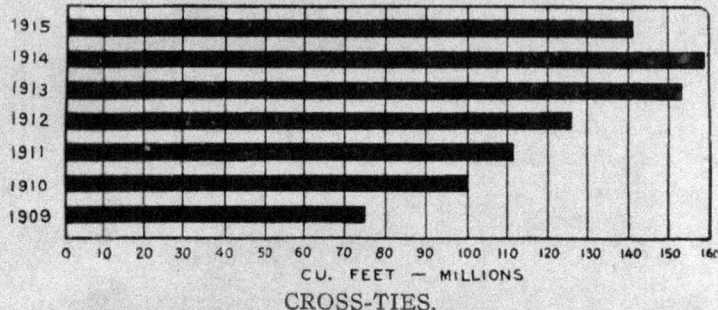

CU. FEET — MILLIONS

CROSS-TIES.

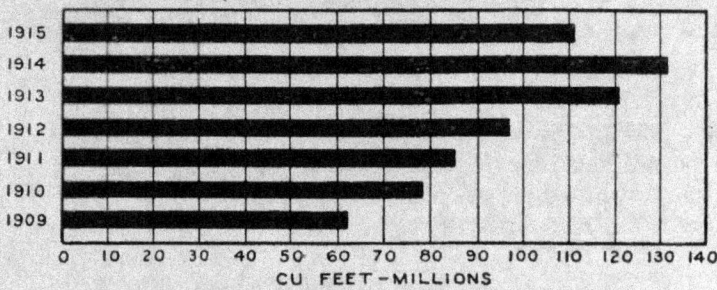

CU FEET—MILLIONS

PILES.

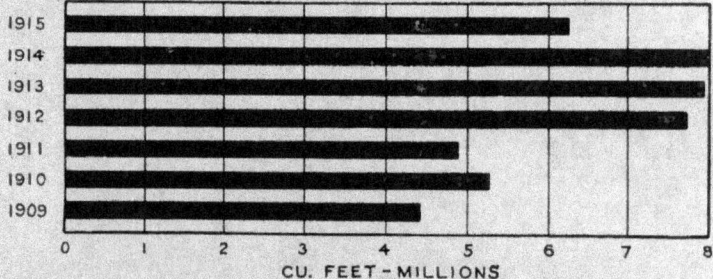

CU. FEET—MILLIONS

POLES.

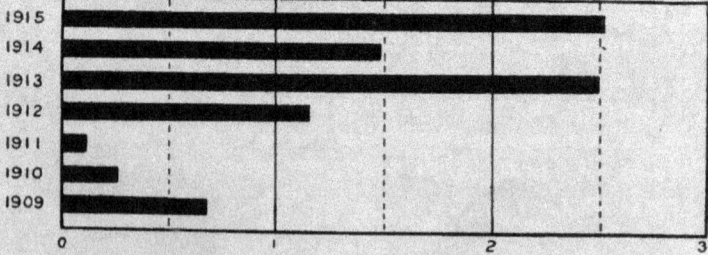

CU FEET—MILLIONS

MATERIAL TREATED IN THE UNITED STATES.

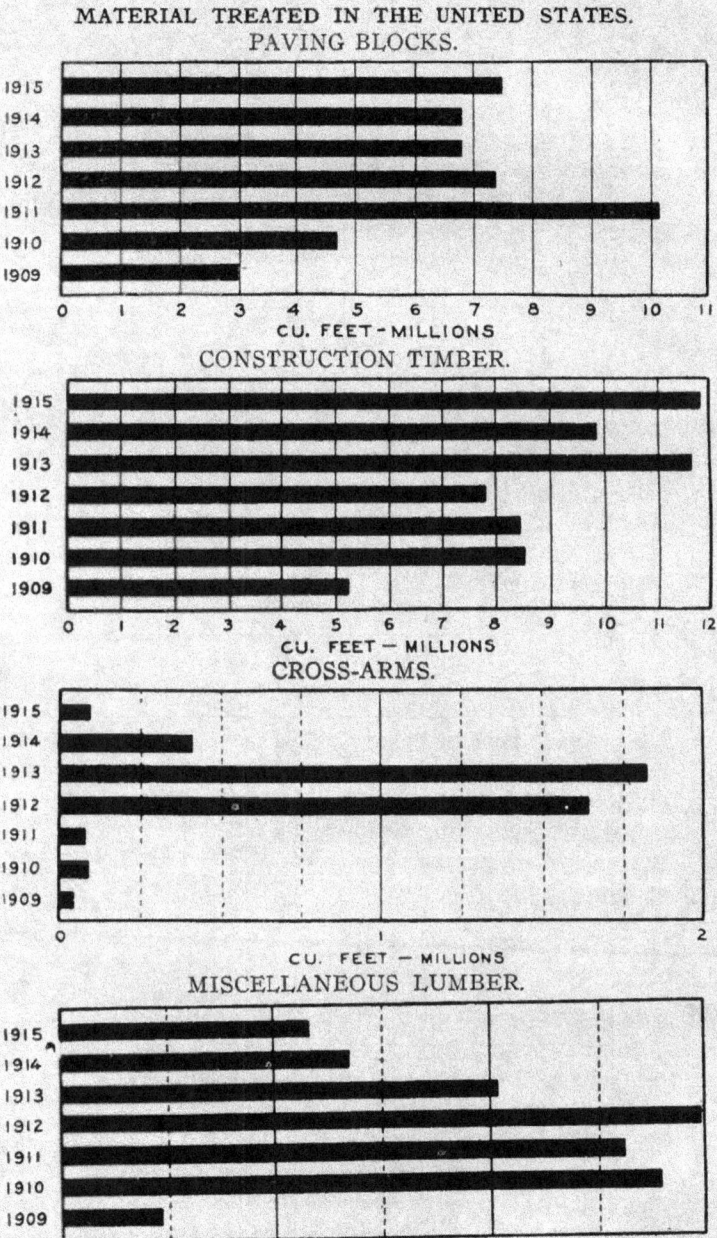

PAVING BLOCKS.

CONSTRUCTION TIMBER.

CROSS-ARMS.

MISCELLANEOUS LUMBER.

CROSS-TIES TREATED IN THE UNITED STATES DURING 1915.

Preservative.	Oak.	Yellow Pine.	Douglas Fir.	Western Pine.	Beech.	Gum.	Tamarack.	Maple.	Birch.	Elm.	Other Kinds.	Total.
Creosote	7,365,673	5,243,516	787,247	301,581	2,469,202	1,650	390,017	36,626	173,916	.....	307,641	17,077,069
Zinc Chloride..	7,954,492	3,257,565	2,760,952	1,702,167	100,000	204,653	449,660	316	55	50,846	1,338,578	17,819,284
Zinc Chloride and Creosote.	1,565,352	40,122	.....	3,861	364,535	71,583	91,496	.....	.....	.....	45,763	2,182,712
Miscellaneous .	.....	.....	5,655	.....	.....	.....	865	.....	.....	.....	.....	6,520
Total	16,885,517	8,541,203	3,553,854	2,007,609	2,933,737	277,886	932,038	36,942	173,971	50,846	1,691,982	37,085,585
Per cent of total treated..	45.53%	23.03%	9.58%	5.42%	7.91%	0.75%	2.51%	0.10%	0.47%	0.14%	4.56%	100.00%

CROSS-TIES TREATED IN THE UNITED STATES.

Year	Number of Miles				Number of Ties Used	Number of Ties Treated	% Treated	Number of Treating Plants In Operation
	STEAM RAILROADS		Horse and Elec. Rwys.	Total				
	Main Tracks	Other Tracks						
1860	30626	3000	200	33826	10147800	} 50,000	0.10	3
1870	52922	9100	1200	63222	18966600			
1880	93267	21977	2000	117244	35173200			
1885	123320	32868	2800	158988	47696400	120000	0.25	5
1886	125185	34441	3120	162746	48823800	510000	1.04	5
1887	137028	37348	3680	178056	53416800	594000	1.11	5
1888	145387	38221	4112	187720	56316000	644000	1.14	6
1889	153725	42242	4930	200897	60269100	615000	1.02	7
1890	163597	42036	5241	213874	64168200	650000	1.01	8
1891	168403	47746	6155	222304	66691200	697000	1.05	8
1892	171564	50787	7040	229391	68817300	790000	1.15	9
1893	176461	53676	8870	239007	71702100	812000	1.13	10
1894	178709	54825	8949	242483	72744900	920000	1.26	11
1895	180657	56237	10810	247704	74311200	1289000	1.73	12
1896	182777	57352	12133	252262	75678600	1307000	1.73	13
1897	183284	58729	13765	255778	76733400	1312000	1.71	13
1898	184648	60686	15942	261276	78382800	1826000	2.33	13
1899	187535	62608	17665	267808	80342400	2510000	3.12	15
1900	192556	66228	19314	278098	83429400	2800000	3.36	15
1901	195562	69790	22217	287569	86270700	4101000	4.75	17
1902	200155	74041	25592	299788	89936400	6180000	6.87	22
1903	205314	78508	27754	311576	93472800	9010000	9.64	27
1904	212243	84830	29548	326621	97986300	12800000	13.06	30
1905	216974	89823	32517	339314	77982000	14890000	19.09	34
1906	222340	94643	36212	353195	102834000	16880000	16.41	39
1907	227455	100520	38812	366787	153700000	19856000	12.92	51
1908	233468	103152	40247	376867	112463000	23776000	21.14	57
1909	236834	106949	40490	384273	123751000	22033000	17.80	68
1910	240293	110936	40088	391317	148231000	30544000	20.60	75
1911	243979	116586	41088	401653	135053000	31141000	23.06	81
1912	246777	121386	42110	410273	123081900	32394000	26.32	87
1913	249777	126038	43043	418858	125657400	40260000	32.04	92
1914	252230	130661	43989	426880	128064000	43847000	34.24	95
1915	255000	135000	44500	434500	130350000	37085585	28.40	102

Mileage of steam railroads from 1890 to 1914 from records of Interstate Commerce Commission.

Cross-ties used and treated from 1906 to 1911 from Census Reports.

Cross-ties used from 1860 to 1905 and from 1912 to 1915 estimated on basis of 300 ties per mile.

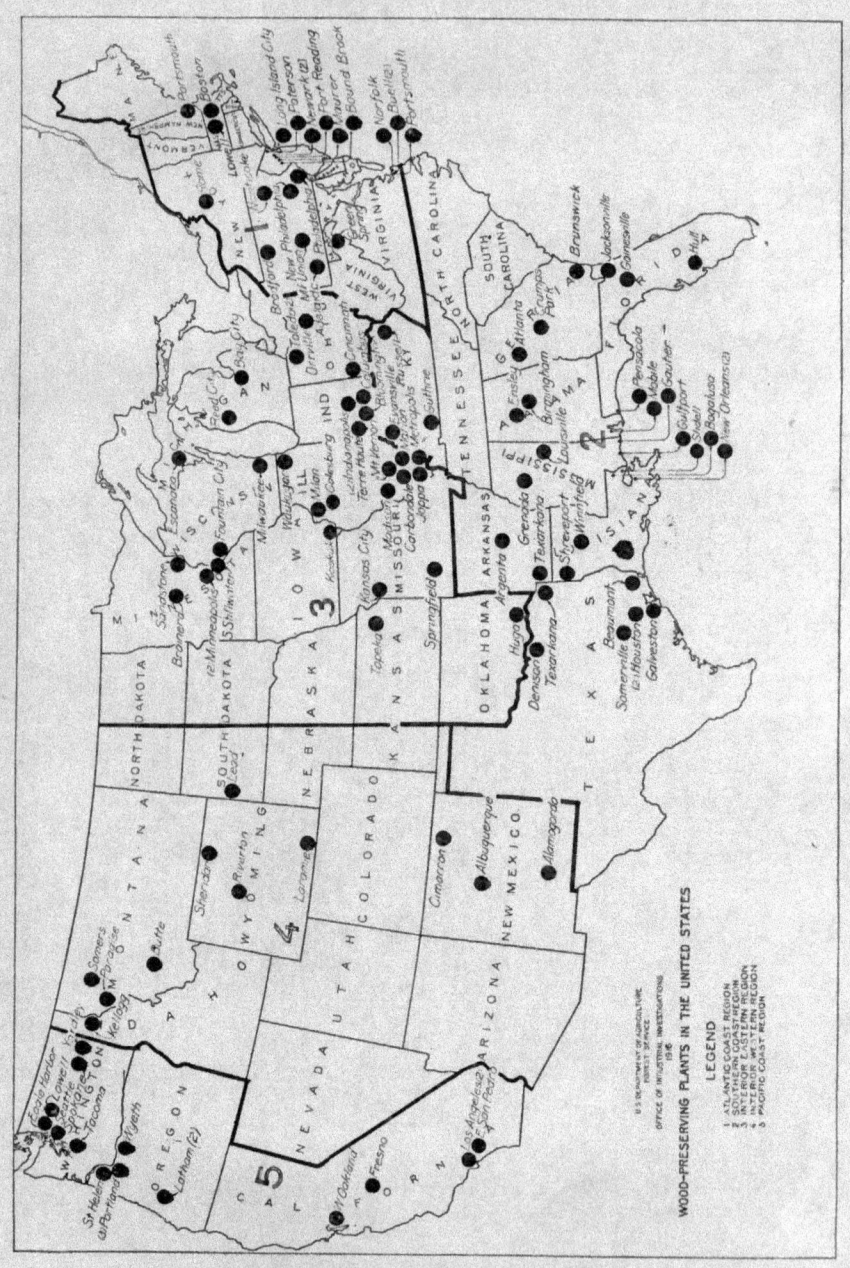

WOOD-PRESERVING PLANTS IN THE UNITED STATES

PROCESSES FOR PRESERVING WOOD.

Inventors have been busy for years endeavoring to find ways and means of protecting wood against decay and from destruction by fire. Although many demonstrations have been made to prove the merits of new processes or preservatives, comparatively few discoveries are ever commercial successes.

The processes of commercial importance are those that either coat a piece of wood with a superficial absorption of preservative, or impregnate the interior of a piece of wood with a preservative under pressure.

In the non-pressure processes the superficial coating of preservative is obtained by brushing or spraying it on, or by dipping or soaking the wood in tanks of the preservative. Where only small lots of material are to be treated and the treated wood will not be abraded or split through the coating of preservative, these processes are economical.

The pressure processes, used wherever large quantities of wood are treated, affect deep penetration of the preservative, thereby protecting the interior of a piece of wood against decay. The depth of penetration attainable is dependent upon a number of factors, chief among which are the kind of wood, the character of its growth, its condition as to seasoning and solidity, the method of treatment, and the preservative used.

The simplest and oldest form of wood preservation is to brush the preservative into the stick to be treated, repeating the application two or more times. A container to hold and in which to heat the preservative is generally necessary. The labor cost of such treatment is comparatively high.

Where wood is in place and brushing preservative on it is inconvenient, spraying it is sometimes adopted. The waste of preservative is against general use of this method of application. Dipping or steeping a piece of wood in open tanks of suitable size, filled with preservatives, will assure a superficial covering with preservative deeper than that to be had by simply brushing on the preservative. The wood is immersed in hot or cold preservative and left to soak up all that it will. Or it is sometimes kept in boiling preservative for several hours and then plunged into cold preservative. In some cases the wood is placed in closed cylinders and the preservative made hot, though no pump pressure is applied. The time of treatment varies greatly, but a hot bath of one to two hours followed by a cool bath of the same period is usually enough. The best results from non-pressure processes are had only when thoroughly-seasoned wood is used. A disadvantage of brush, spray, and open-tank treatment is the loss of preservative through evaporation.

The locations of many non-pressure plants are given on page 40. Details as to the erection of similar plants may be had from the manufacturers listed on page 35. Particulars as to methods of treatment may be had from the purveyors of preservatives listed on page 30.

The general method of impregnating wood with a preservative is in cylinders, which range in size from 72 inches in diameter and 42 feet long to 108 inches in diameter and 172 feet long. The preservative is forcibly injected into the wood by means of pumps.

The two leading preservatives used in the pressure processes are creosote and zinc chloride, either alone or together, and the absorption per cubic foot of wood treated varies from 2 to 20 pounds of creosote, and usually from 0.5 to 0.75 ℔. dry zinc chloride. The maximum quantity of creosote is usually injected into piles and other marine timbers that are subject to attack of the teredo and other marine borers; in land situations where decay is the principal source of failure about one-half as much creosote is injected into the wood. Zinc chloride is best adapted to timber for use in arid or semi-arid regions, where precipitation is too low to leach out the preservative, and where low first cost is essential. The pressure processes are divided into:

(1). Full-Cell treatments, which force into and leave in wood practically all the preservative it will hold where penetrated, thereby giving maximum protection against decay for that depth of penetration; and

(2). Empty-Cell treatments, which aim to reduce materially the final retention of preservative, while not reducing the depth of penetration.

Either green or seasoned timber can be treated by the pressure processes. When green timber is put into the cylinder it is often seasoned by means of live steam, followed by a vacuum to dry the wood before treatment. A vacuum is also drawn at the end of the treatment to hasten the draining of the surplus from the cylinder and to dry the timber.

The better-known pressure processes used in the United States are:

Bethell.—*(Full-Cell Process.)*

Patented by John Bethell in England in 1838. Commonly used for the treatment of piles, poles, cross-arms, paving blocks, structural timbers, lumber, and ties. Consists essentially of the following steps:

a. Preliminary vacuum one-half to one or more hours.

b. Oil injected under pressure, maximum usually between 100 and 180 ℔s. per square inch.

c. Final vacuum (sometimes omitted).

Green timber is usually subjected to a live steam bath at about 20 ℔s. pressure for several hours before the preliminary vacuum. Seasoned timber is not usually steamed in this process, except in the case of paving blocks. The amount of oil injected depends upon the specifications of the purchaser, but the absorption per cubic foot is usually within the following ranges:

Lumber, poles, structural timbers, cross-arms, ties, fresh-water and land piles, 8 to 12 pounds.
Paving blocks, 12 to 20 pounds.
Salt water piles, 16 to 24 pounds.

Boiling.

Patented by W. G. Curtis and John D. Isaacs in 1895 and reissued the same year. (U. S. patent 545,222, and reissue 11,515).

Used chiefly for creosoting Douglas fir piles, timber, lumber, ties, and paving blocks. Consists essentially of the following steps:

a. Wood (either green or seasoned) in the retort is covered with oil at about 160° F.

b. Oil heated to 225° to 250° F. at atmospheric pressure and vapors passed through a condenser.

c. Heating continued until rate of condensation falls to 1/6 to 1/10 of a pound of water per cubic foot of wood per hour. This frequently requires 40 to 60 hours for green timber, and sometimes more.

d. Retort filled with cool oil, allowing temperature to fall.

e. Pressure applied, maximum 120 to 150 lbs. per square inch, until desired absorption obtained; usually 10 to 12 lbs. per cubic foot.

Boulton.—*(Boiling Under Vacuum.)*

Patented by S. B. Boulton in England and the United States. (See U. S. patent 247,602, issued Sept. 27, 1881), also by O. P. M. Goss in the United States. (See U. S. patent 1,167,492, issued in 1916).

Used chiefly for the treatment of Douglas fir piles, timber, ties, lumber and paving blocks. Consists essentially of the following steps:

a. Timber immersed in hot creosote and subjected to a vacuum, and the escaping vapors drawn through a condenser.

b. Temperature (usually 190° F. to 210° F.) and vacuum maintained until the rate of condensation of water falls to a specified amount per cubic foot of wood per hour, usually 1/6 to 1/10 of a pound.

c. Vacuum discontinued and pressure applied until desired absorption obtained.

The object of the vacuum is to evaporate the water from the wood at a lower temperature than in the ordinary steaming or straight-boiling process.

Burnett.

Patented in England in 1838 by William Burnett.

In general use for treating ties, lumber and timber with zinc chloride. Consists essentially as follows for seasoned wood:

a. Preliminary vacuum.

b. Zinc chloride solution applied under pressure of 100 to 175 ℔s. per square inch, to approximate refusal.

For green timber a steaming period of one to five or more hours at about 20 ℔s. is usually applied before the vacuum. The strength of the zinc solution generally is so regulated that at refusal the timber will have absorbed from ¼ to ½ ℔., usually the latter, of dry zinc chloride per cubic foot.

Card.

Patented by J. B. Card in 1906, (U. S. patent 815,404). Used chiefly for ties, lumber, and timbers. The essential parts of the process are:

a. The use of a mixture containing about 80% of zinc chloride solution and 20% creosote.

b. The method of keeping the zinc chloride and creosote mixed during treatment by means of a rotary pump, which draws the mixture from the top of the retort and returns it at the bottom through a perforated pipe.

The use of steaming, vacuum, and pressure are the same as in the Bethell process. It is customary to inject about ½ ℔. of zinc chloride and 2 to 3 ℔s. of creosote per cubic foot.

Lowry.—*(Empty-Cell Process.)*

Patented by C. B. Lowry in 1906. (U. S. patent 831,450). Used chiefly for creosoting air-seasoned cross-ties. Consists essentially of the following steps:

a. Without first drawing a vacuum, creosote at not to exceed 200° F. is injected into the wood to refusal, or to a specific amount.

b. A quick vacuum is drawn to remove the excess oil from the timber.

The air imprisoned by injecting the oil without a preliminary vacuum expands during the final vacuum, forcing out a certain amount of the oil with it. The process is classed as an empty-cell process for this reason. The net absorption is from 6-8 pounds per cubic foot.

Rueping.—*(Empty-Cell Process.)*

Patented in the United States in 1902 by Max Rueping. (U. S. patents 707,799 and 709,799). The second patent was reissued October, 1907. (Reissue 12,707).

Used chiefly for ties and lumber. Consists of the following steps:

a. Retort, containing the wood, is filled with compressed air; the pressure varying with the kind and condition of the wood.

b. Oil forced into retort, gradually allowing air to escape, but without reducing pressure.

c. When retort is full of oil, pressure is increased to a maximum of 150 to 200 ℔s. per square inch, and held to refusal, or until specified absorption is obtained.

d. Oil drained and vacuum drawn to remove excess of oil from the wood.

If green timber is treated, it is first artificially seasoned by steaming, boiling, or boiling under vacuum, before the air pressure is applied. Net absorption usually 4 to 6 lbs. per cubic foot.

Steaming.—*(Colman Process.)*

Not patented.

Used almost exclusively for the treatment of Douglas fir piles. Consists essentially of the following steps:

a. Timber steamed at a pressure of 90 to 100 lbs. per square inch for 3 to 10 hours.

b. Steam released and vacuum drawn until timber is considered seasoned. This sometimes requires 18 to 20 hours. The temperature within the retort during the vacuum period is usually maintained above 200° F.

c. Oil is injected at a maximum pressure of 100 to 150 lbs. per square inch until desired absorption is obtained.

There are many other processes, the merits and demerits of which have been or are yet to be demonstrated. Most wood-preserving plants are equipped to treat by any processes desired by the user of the treated wood. They also may be relied upon to advise the kinds of treatments which will bring results to which they can point later with satisfaction.

Conservation by preservation is economy exemplified.

WOOD PRESERVATIVES.

The substances proposed as a means of protecting wood against destruction by fire, fungi, insects, or worms, include the following:

Aluminum sulphate.
Animal oils.
Barium carbonate.
Barium sulphate.
Borax.
Cedar oil.
Copper sulphate.
Creosotes (coal-tar, water-gas-tar, wood, petroleum.)
Crude oil.
Fish oil.
Glue.
Gums (various.)
Iron sulphate.
Lime hydrate.
Linseed oil.
Magnesium sulphate.
Mercuric chloride.
Molasses and low syrups.

Petroleum oils.
Potassium carbonate.
Potassium nitrate.
Resins.
Sodium carbonate.
Sodium chloride.
Sodium fluoride.
Sodium muriate.
Sodium sulphate.
Sulphuric acid.
Tannin.
Tar.
Tartaric acid.
Vegetable oils.
Wax.
Whale oil.
Zinc chloride.
Zinc sulphate.

The merit of a wood preservative is determined either by its ability to poison fungi or bacteria, or to waterproof wood. Preservatives vary greatly in their toxicity (property to poison), and the greater their toxicity the longer will the wood keep sound. Toxic preservatives that will easily penetrate wood, do not affect its strength, and are obtainable at a reasonable price, are the most efficient and economical.

The consumption of wood preservatives in the United States for a series of years is given in the accompanying table.

WOOD PRESERVATIVES USED IN THE UNITED STATES.

Year	Number of Plants	Creosote. Gallons.	Zinc Chloride. Pounds.	Other Preservatives. Gallons*.
1909	64	51,431,212	16,215,109	†
1910	71	63,266,271	16,802,532	2,333,707
1911	80	73,027,335	16,359,797	1,000,000
1912	84	83,666,490	20,751,711	3,072,462
1913	93	108,373,359	26,466,803	3,885,738
1914	94	79,334,606	27,212,259	{ 9,429,444‡ { 2,486,637
1915	102	80,859,442	33,269,604	{ 3,205,563‡ { 1,693,544

*Includes crude oil, coke oven-tar, refined coal-tar and carbolineum oils.
†Statistics not available.
‡"Paving oil."

Some preservatives like zinc chloride, mercuric chloride, and copper sulphate, are made from inorganic compounds which are soluble in

water, and these will leach out of the wood when it is exposed to very
wet surroundings. In dry localities, however, these inorganic preservatives will assure a considerably longer life to treated wood than
could be expected of the untreated wood. Other preservatives, such
as the creosotes, which are made from organic compounds, are more
waterproof and less volatile.

Creosote.

The creosote suitable for preserving wood is derived from the tar
obtained in the destructive distillation of wood, coal, petroleum, etc.
Creosote oil, in the scientific sense, may be defined as any and all
distillate oils boiling between 200° and 400° Centigrade, which are obtained by distillation from tars consisting principally of compounds
belonging to the aromatic series and containing well-defined amounts
of phenoloids.

Creosote is the most important wood preservative, and has been
in use for this purpose for a great many years. The consumption
of creosote oil in the United States in the five years from 1909 to 1913
more than doubled, and in the seven years from 1909 to 1915 was as
follows:

CREOSOTE USED IN THE UNITED STATES.

Year	Total Creosote Used.	Domestic Creosote.	Per Cent of Total	Imported Creosote.	Per Cent of Total
	Gallons.	Gallons.		Gallons.	
1909	51,426,212	13,862,171	27	37,569,041	73
1910	63,266,271	18,184,355	29	45,081,916	71
1911	73,027,335	21,510,629	29	51,516,706	71
1912	83,666,490	31,135,195	37	52,531,295	63
1913	108,373,359	41,700,167	38	66,673,192	62
1914	79,334,606	28,026,870	35	51,307,736	65
1915	80,859,442	43,358,435*	54	37,501,007	46

*41,333,890 gals. coal-tar and 2,024,545 gals. water-gas-tar.

The domestic production of creosote oil has grown steadily,
especially since the European war interfered with exports to the
United States. In 1914 the production of creosote oil in the United
States amounted to 28,026,870 gallons, and a year later had nearly
doubled to 43,358,435 gallons. Domestic manufacturers furnished 35%
of the total amount of creosote oil used in 1914, and in 1915 they sup-
plied 54%. The imports in 1914 amounted to 65% of the total consumption of creosote oil in the United States, and in 1915 the foreign
supply fell to 46%.

Specifications for coal-tar creosote oil, calculated on the basis
of the dry oil when distilled by the common method (using an 8-oz.
retort, asbestos covered, with standard thermometer, bulb ½ in.

above the surface of the oil), prepared by the American Railway Engineering Association, are as follows:

Distillation	Grade 1.	Grade 2.	Grade 3.
Below 210° C..............	5%	8%	10%
" 235° C.....Not over	25%	35%	40%
Residue above 355° C. Over	5%—soft	5%—soft	5%—soft
Water ....Not over	3%	3%	3%
Specific gravity at 38° C....	1.03	1.03	1.025

Grade 1 oil shall be a pure product obtained from coal-gas-tar or coke-oven-tar, and shall be free from any tar, including coal-gas-tar and coke-oven-tar, oil or residue obtained from petroleum or any other source; it shall be completely liquid at 38° C., and shall be free from suspended matter. Oils 2 and 3 shall be the best-obtainable grades of coal-tar creosote.

The specifications for creosote oil prepared in behalf of the American Society of Municipal Improvements in October, 1916, by that association's Committee on Standard Specifications for Creosoted Wood Block Paving, are as follows:

"A" Coal-Tar Paving Oil: A coal-tar product at least 65% a distillate of coal-gas tar or coke-oven tar; the remainder refined or filtered coal-gas tar or coke-oven tar.

"B" Coal-Tar Distillate Oil: A distillate of coal-gas tar or coke-oven tar.

	"A"	"B"
Water	Not more than 3%......	Not more than 3%
Matter insoluble in benzol	Not more than 3%......	Not more than 0.5%
Specific gravity at 38° C.	Between 1.07 and 1.12...	Not less than 1.06
Distillates		
Up to 210° C.......	Not over 5%..........	Not over 5%
Up to 235° C.......	Not over 25%..........	Not over 15%
Residue above 355° C...	If over 35% shall have float test of not over 80 sec. at 70° C.....	If over 10% shall have float test of not over 50 sec. at 70° C.
Specific gravity of fraction between 235° C and 315° C.............	Not less than 1.02 at 38°/15.5° C............	Not less than 1.02 at 38°/15.5° C.
Specific gravity of fraction between 315° C and 355° C.............	Not less than 1.09 at 38°/15.5° C............	Not less than 1.09 at 38°/15.5° C.
Coke residue	Not more than 10%.....	Not more than 2%

Zinc Chloride.

The principal water-soluble salt which is used as an antiseptic for destroying fungi that attack wood in localities that are not excessively wet is zinc chloride, which has been employed as a wood preservative for nearly forty years. It is purchased either in the fused state or in a concentrated solution. Fused zinc chloride should contain at least 94% of water-soluble chloride of zinc, and be free from acids. It should be practically free from soluble iron or other inorganic impurities insoluble in hydrochloric acid. The concentrated solution contains about 50% water, and this is the form in which zinc chloride is injected into wood. The consumption of zinc chloride in the United States for preserving wood amounted in 1914 to 27,212,259 pounds, and in 1915 to 33,269,604 pounds.

A number of patented, proprietary wood preservatives are being marketed. They are used generally in gallon or barrel lots in localities near their points of manufacture, to minimize the cost of their transportation.

MANUFACTURERS OF OR DEALERS IN WOOD PRESERVATIVES.

Creosote.

UNITED STATES.

American Tar Products Co., 208 La Salle St., Chicago, Ill.; Milwaukee, Wis.; St. Louis, Mo.; Steubenville, O.; Woodward, Ala.; Youngstown, O.

Armitage Mfg. Co., 2716 E. Grace St., Richmond, Va.

Barnaby & Co., Colman Bldg., Seattle, Wash.

Barrett Co., The, 17 Battery Place, New York; Birmingham, Ala.; Boston, Mass.; Chicago, Ill.; Cincinnati, O.; Cleveland, O.; Detroit, Mich.; Kansas City, Mo.; Louisville, Ky.; Minneapolis, Minn.; Nashville, Tenn.; New Orleans, La.; Peoria, Ill.; Philadelphia, Pa.; Pittsburgh, Pa.; St. Louis, Mo.; Salt Lake City, Utah; Seattle, Wash.

Carolina Portland Cement Co., New Orleans, La.

Chatfield Mfg. Co., Cincinnati, O.

Cleveland-Cliffs Iron Co., Cleveland, O.

Creosote Supply Co., 1105 Queen & Crescent Bldg., New Orleans, La.

Denver Gas and Electric Light Co., 900 15th St., Denver, Colo.

Lembcke, von Bernuth Co., 171 Madison Avenue, New York.

Lewis Mfg. Co., F. J., Chicago, Ill.; Birmingham, Ala.; Moline, Ill.

Nashville Chemical Co., Nashville, Tenn.

Republic Creosoting Co., Indianapolis, Ind.; Minneapolis, Minn.; Mobile, Ala.

Semet-Solvay Co., Syracuse, N. Y.

United Gas Improvement Co., Philadelphia, Pa.

Utah Light & Power Co., Ogden, Utah.

Warren Brothers, Cambridge, Mass.

Zopher Mills, 91 Pioneer St., Brooklyn, N. Y.

FOREIGN.

American Tar Products Co., Montreal, Canada.

Blagden, Waugh & Co., London, England.

British Creosote Co. (Shields & Ramsay, Agents), Glasgow, Scotland.

Brotherton & Co., Ltd., Leeds, England.

Burt, Bolton & Haywood, Ltd., London, England.

Chemische Fabrik Grunan, Grunan (Berlin), Germany.

Chemische Fabrik Ladenburg, Ladenburg, Germany.

Dominion Tar & Chemical Co., Sydney, Nova Scotia.

Dunn Bros. & Co., Manchester, England.

Forbes, Abbott & Leonard, London, England.

Gas Light & Coke Co., London, England.

Graesser, R., Ruabon, Wales.

Hird, Hastie & Co., Glasgow, Scotland.

Leitch & Co., John W., Heddersfield, England.

Creosote—(Continued).

Lowe & Co., Chas., London, England.

Major & Co., Hull, England.

Metcalf, J., Altham (Near Accrington), England.

Munro Co., Robt. A., Ltd., Glasgow, Scotland.

Page & Co., Chas., London, England.

Raschig, Dr. F., Ludwigshafen on Rhein, Germany.

South Metropolitan Gas Works, London, England.

Tennant & Co., Chas., London, England.

Tullock Co., Wm., Glasgow, Scotland.

Zinc Chloride.

Commercial Acid Co., St. Louis, Mo.

General Chemical Co., 112 W. Adams St., Chicago, Ill.

Grasselli Chemical Co., Cleveland, O.

Patented Proprietary Preservatives.

Aczol. J. Gerlache, Boulevard du Nord, 68, Brussels, Belgium.

Atlas "A." Atlas Preservative Co., New York.

Aztec. Interocean Oil Co., New York.

Avenarius Carbolineum. Carbolineum Wood Preserving Co., Milwaukee, Wis., New York.

Barol. Anthrol Wood Preserving Co., New York.

Barrett Grade One Liquid Creosote Oil (Carbosota). The Barrett Co., 17 Battery Place, New York; Birmingham, Ala.; Boston, Mass.; Chicago, Ill.; Cincinnati, O.; Cleveland, O.; Detroit, Mich.; Kansas City, Mo.; Louisville, Ky.; Minneapolis, Minn.; Nashville, Tenn.; New Orleans, La.; Peoria, Ill.; Philadelphia, Pa.; Pittsburgh, Pa.; St. Louis, Mo.; Salt Lake City, Utah; Seattle, Wash.

Beechwood Creosote. Lake Superior Iron and Chemical Co., Detroit, Mich.

B. M. Franz Workman, New York.

Carbolite Carbolineum. The Dominion Paving & Contracting Co., 55 Gore Vale Ave., Toronto, Ont.

Carbosota. The Barrett Co. (See above.)

C-A-Wood-Preserver. C-A-Wood-Preserver Co., Inc., St. Louis, Mo.

Chlorocene. Sherwin-Williams Co., Cleveland, O.

Concentrol. F. & H. Aldred, Derby, England.

Conservo. Samuel Cabot, Inc., Boston, Mass.

Copper Sulphate. American Smelting & Refining Co., New York. General Chemical Co., 112 W. Adams St., Chicago, Ill.

Copperized Oil. Copper Oil Products Co., New York.

Corrosive Sublimate. Roessler & Hasslacher Chemical Co., New York.

Cresol-Calcium. Blagden, Waugh & Co., London, England.

Eternoid. L. & M. Supply and Equipment Co., Trenton, N. J.

Ferrosote. National Wood Preserving & Lumber Co., Chicago, Ill.

Grade One Liquid Creosote. The Barrett Co. (See above.)

Holz-Helfer. Vaughn Paint Co., Cleveland, O.

Kreodone. Republic Creosoting Co., Indianapolis, Ind.; Minneapolis, Minn.; Mobile, Ala.

Letteney. The Northeastern Co., 6 Beacon St., Boston, Mass.

Locustine. W. H. Huff, Beverly, N. J.

Montanin. Montanin Co., New York.

Mykantin. Farbwerke Hoechst Co., San Francisco, Cal.

Para-Kresol. American Chemical & Textile Co., Wilmington, N. C.

Penetin. Preservative Materials Co., New York.

Preservol. Newbold Mfg. Co., 135 Greenwich St., New York.

Pyrolin. Pyrolin Products Co., Inc., Fort Dodge, Iowa.

Reeves' Wood-Preserver. The Reeves Co., New Orleans, La.

Sapwood Antiseptic. J. W. Long, Chicago, Ill.

Saum's Preservative. Geo. W. Saums Co., Trenton, N. J.

Sodium Fluoride. General Chemical Co., Pittsburgh, Pa. Harshaw, Fuller & Goodwin Co., Cleveland, O.

Sodium Silicate. General Chemical Co., 112 W. Adams St., Chicago, Ill.

Solignum. The Northeastern Company, Boston, Mass.

S. P. F. Carbolineum. S. P. F. Wood-Preserving Co., New York.

Spirittine. Spirittine Chemical Co., Wilmington, N. C.

Timberasphalt. Indian Refining Co., New York.

Zinc Sulphate. General Chemical Co., 112 W. Adams St., Chicago, Ill. Grasselli Chemical Co., Cleveland, O.

Pavements of preserved wood
are pavements of permanent worth.

USES OF PRESERVED WOOD.

Wood has many advantages over its substitutes; namely:

Wood is widely distributed and easily obtainable.

Wood can be worked easily into any shape with simple tools.

Wood is strong, tough, elastic and noiseless.

Wood will not contract or expand under varying temperatures.

Wood is a non-conductor of heat and electricity.

Wood used in structures or for other purposes can be more easily removed and used over again than equally-substantial material.

Preservative treatment gives to wood the additional advantage of durability wherever decay is a factor in its service.

The principal uses of treated wood are:

Cross-Ties.	Cross-Arms.
Switch-Ties.	Fence Posts.
Bridge-Ties.	Blocks for Paving
Structural Timbers.	and Flooring.
Piles.	Miscellaneous Lumber.
Poles.	

One-third of all the railway ties used annually are now treated with preservatives, and the consumption of treated wood for railway work is steadily increasing.

Treated telegraph and telephone poles and cross-arms are now the rule rather than the exception. Only creosoted piles will withstand the attack of marine borers, and in consequence untreated wood is now rarely found in wharf supports.

Streets paved with wood blocks are no longer uncommon. Their growing popularity is justified by their wearability, noiselessness, dustlessness, etc.

As flooring, wood block is used in:

Foundries.	Ferryboats and Approaches.	Rubber Factories.
Machine Shops (all kinds).	Driveways.	Hospitals.
Shops Handling Heavy Machinery.	Bridges.	Laundries.
Railway Shops.	Post Offices.	Printing Establishments.
Railway Stations.	Dumping Platforms.	Garages.
Warehouses.	Freight Platforms.	Cotton Mills.
Factories.	Loading Platforms.	Paper Mills.
Factory Courts.	Station Platforms.	Kitchens.
Freight Houses.	Wharves and Docks.	Bakeries.
Express Rooms.	Barns.	Engine Houses.
Baggage Rooms.	Tennis Courts.	Milk Depots.
Wild Animal Cages, Runways, etc.	Stables.	Breweries.
	Slaughter Houses.	Dairies.

Satisfied users replied as follows when asked why they preferred wood block as flooring:

Wears well; durable; long life.
Easy on feet of workmen; men like to work on these floors.
Quiet; noiseless.
Easily repaired.
Low upkeep cost.
Smooth, easy trucking; good surface.
Good footing. Not slippery.
Saves tools dropped, castings, fine work, materials, kegs, etc.
Sanitary.
Warm.
Dustless; clean.
Easily cleaned.
Resilient, pliable, shock absorber.
Easy on mules and horses.
Easy to move or set up machinery on, to put in pipes, etc.
Saves trucks.
Non-inflammable.
Stands great abuse.
Dries quickly; waterproof.
Makes a solid floor.
Non-absorbent.
Does not crack or chip when heavy castings are thrown on floor.
Makes a neat floor.
Keeps a neat floor.
Keeps out flies, mosquitoes, etc.
Not damaged by metal grinding into the floor.
Easily laid.

Preserved structural timbers and miscellaneous lumber are used for numerous purposes about the farm, in silos, barns, stock pens, chicken coops, fencing, culverts, etc.; about mills, as sills, posts, rafters, conduits, etc.; in mines, as supports, etc.

Preserved piles are practically permanent.

MANUFACTURERS OF WOOD-PRESERVING EQUIPMENT.

Allis-Chalmers Mfg. Co.............................Milwaukee, Wis.
Brown Hoisting Machinery Co.........................Cleveland, O.
Bovaird & Seyfaud Mfg. Co...........................Bradford, Pa.
Casey & Hedges...................................Chattanooga, Tenn.
Chicago Bridge & Iron Co..............................Chicago, Ill.
Crane Co..Chicago, Ill.
Coeur d'Alene Iron Works.........................Wallace, Idaho.
Crook, Kries & Co., (Successors to T. C. Basshor Co.), Baltimore, Md.
Fairbanks-Morse Co................................St. Paul, Minn.
Foxboro Co., The...................................Foxboro, Mass.
Graver Tank Works, Wm.........................East Chicago, Ind.
Gravier Tank Works................................Galveston, Tex.
Greenlee Bros. & Co..................................Rockford, Ill.
Hilke Stacker Co..................................New York, N. Y.
International Creosoting & Construction Co...........Galveston, Tex.
Jacobs & Sons, S..................................Birmingham, Ala.
Lakewood Engineering Co.............................Cleveland, O.
Logan Iron Works...................................Brooklyn, N. Y.
Manitowoc Engineering Works.....................Manitowoc, Wis.
Mathews Gravity Carrier Co.......................Ellwood City, Pa.
Mohr & Sons, John.....................................Chicago, Ill.
Moran Bros...Seattle, Wash.
National Boiler & Sheet Iron Works...............Indianapolis, Ind.
Orenstein-Arthur Koppel Co.........................New York, N. Y.
Payne & Joubert......................................New Orleans, La.
Petroleum Iron Works..................................Sharon, Pa.
Reeves Bros. Co.......................................Alliance, O.
Schaeffer & Budenberg Mfg. Co.....................Brooklyn, N. Y.
Struther-Wells Co..Warren, Pa.
Taylor Instrument Companies........................Rochester, N. Y.
Union Iron Works..................................San Francisco, Cal.
Willamette Iron and Steel Works...................Portland, Oregon.
Worthington Pump and Machinery Corporation.......New York, N. Y.
Yeomans Bros. Co.....................................Chicago, Ill.

Treated ties typify tip-top track.

USERS OF PRESERVED WOOD.

With a wider knowledge of the merits of treated wood for many purposes, and its greater economy as compared with the natural product, has come a more liberal demand for treated wood, especially from the larger users of this material. To name every user of treated wood would be quite a task, but it is possible to give some idea of the industries that absorb the increasing supply, as mentioned below:

Treated Cross-Ties, Switch-Ties and Bridge Ties.
Railroad companies.

Treated Structural Timbers.
Manufacturing companies.
Mining companies.
Railroad companies.
Agriculturists.

Treated Piles.
Railroad companies.
Shipbuilding companies.
Dock companies.
U. S. Government.
Municipalities.

Treated Poles and Cross-Arms.
Telegraph companies.
Telephone companies.
Railroad companies.
Light companies.
Power companies.
Water supply companies.

Treated Fence Posts.
Railroad companies.
Agriculturists.

Treated Miscellaneous Lumber.
Railroad companies.
Agriculturists.
Shipbuilding companies.

Treated Wood Blocks.

Railroad companies.
Express companies.
Manufacturing companies.
Foundries.
Machine shops.
Post offices.
Garages.
Dock companies.
Shipbuilding companies.
Cotton mills.
Paper mills.
Slaughter houses.
Stables.
Platforms.

Hospitals.
Print shops.
Laundries.
Hotels and restaurants.
Bakeries.
Dairies.
Warehouses.
Stores.
Engine houses.
Breweries.
Rubber works.
Menageries.
Freight houses.
Barns.

WOOD-PRESERVING PLANTS,
UNITED STATES, CANADA AND MEXICO.
PRESSURE PROCESSES.
UNITED STATES.

Managing Company	Headquarters	Location of Plant	Year Built	Retorts		
				No.	Diam. In.	Length Ft.
American Creosoting Co.	New York, N. Y.	Newark, N. J.	1906	1	78	105
				1	78	165
" " "	Louisville, Ky.	Indianapolis, Ind.	1913	2	64	134
" " "	" "	Marion, Ill.	1907	2	84	134
" " "	" "	Springfield, Mo.	1907	2	84	134
" " "	" "	Kansas City, Mo.	1907	2	84	134
" " "	" "	Russell, Ky.	1915	1	84	134
" " "	" "	Hugo, Okla.	1907	2	84	134
American Creosote Works.	New Orleans, La.	Southport, nr. New Orleans	1901	1	84	172
				1	108	172
" " "	" " "	Louisville, Miss.	1912	1	108	172
Anaconda Copper Mining Co.	Butte, Mont.	Butte, Mont.	1910	1	72	43
A. T. & S. F. Rwy. Co.	Topeka, Kan.	Somerville, Tex.	1906	5	74	132
" " " "	" "	Albuquerque, N. M.	1908	2	74	132
Atlantic Coast Line R. R. Co.	Wilmington, N. C.	Gainesville, Fla.	1912	2	74	138
Atlantic Creo. & W. P. Wks.	Norfolk, Va.	Norfolk, Va.	1901	1	78	62
				1	78	82
				1	78	126
Ayer & Lord Tie Co.	Chicago, Ill.	Grenada, Miss.	1904	4	74	128
" " " "	" "	Argenta, Ark.	1907	4	74	132
" " " "	" "	Carbondale, Ill.	1902	4	72	122
				4	74	132
Baltimore & Ohio R. R. Co.	Baltimore, Md.	Green Spring, W. Va.	1912	2	84	132
Barber Asphalt Paving Co.	Maurer, N. J.	Maurer, N. J.	1905	4	72	115
Boston Elevated Rwy. Co.	Boston, Mass.	South Boston, Mass.	1916	1	90	51
Buffalo, Rochester & Pitsburgh R. R. Co.	Rochester, N. Y.	Bradford, Pa.	1910	1	75	95
Bunker Hill & Sullivan Mg. Co.	Kellogg, Idaho	Kellogg, Idaho	1908	1	84	10
Carbolineum Wood Pres. Co.	Portland, Ore.	Portland, Ore.	1901	1	..	...
Central of Ga. R. R. Co.	Macon, Ga.	Macon, Ga.	1912	2	84	116
Central R. R. of New Jersey.	Port Reading, N. J.	Port Reading, N. J.	1912	2	88	140
Charlotte Harbor & No. Ry. Co.	Boca Grande, Fla.	Hull, Fla.	1912	1	74	73
C. B. & Q. R. R. Co.	Galesburg, Ill.	Galesburg, Ill.	1907	5	74	132
" " "	Chicago, Ill.	Sheridan, Wyo.	1899	2	74	132
Chicago Creosoting Co.	Chicago, Ill.	Waukegan, Ill.	1907	2	72	134
" " "	" "	Terre Haute, Ind.	1912	2	132	20
Chicago & N. W. Ry. Co.	" "	Escanaba, Mich.	1903	3	72	112
" " " "	" "	Riverton, Wyo.	1915	1	72	110
Colman Co., J. M.	Seattle, Wash.	Seattle, Wash.	1884	3	75	120
Colonial Creosoting Co.	Louisville, Ky.	Bogalusa, La.	1912	2	72	134
Columbia Creosoting Co.	Portland, Oregon	Linnton, nr. P'tland, Ore.	1912	1	72	132
				1	72	65
Compressed Wood Preserving Co.	Cincinnati, O.	Cincinnati, O.	1909	2	72	76
Continental Tie & Lbr. Co.	Denver, Colo.	Cimarron, N. M.	1913	1	84	87
El Paso & S. W. R. R. Co.	El Paso, Tex.	Alamogordo, N. M.	1902	2	72	106
Eppinger & Russell Co.	New York, N. Y.	Long Island City, N. Y.	1878	4	72	100

WOOD-PRESERVING PLANTS IN UNITED STATES—(Continued).

Managing Company	Headquarters	Location of Plant	Year Built	No.	Diam. In.	Length Ft.
Eppinger & Russell Co.	New York, N. Y.	Jacksonville, Fla.	1909	3	84	130
Federal Creosoting Co.	Louisville, Ky.	Bound Brook, N. J.	1909	1	84	150
" " "	" "	Toledo, O.	1909	3	84	134
" " "	" "	Rome, N. Y.	1910	2	84	150
" " "	" "	Paterson, N. J.	1909	1	84	150
Georgia Creosoting Co.	Louisville, Ky.	Brunswick, Ga.	1915	2	84	121
Great Northern Ry. Co.	St. Paul, Minn.	Somers, Mont.	1901	4	72	110
Gulfport Creosoting Co.	Gulfport, Miss.	Gulfport, Miss.	1906	2	84	120
Indiana Creosoting Co.	Louisville, Ky.	Bloomington, Ind.	1907	1	84	134
Indiana Tie Co.	Evansville, Ind.	Evansville, Ind.	1907	2	72	110
" " "	Evansville, Ind.	Joppa, Ill.	1909	2	72	110
Indiana Zinc Creosoting Co.	Terre Haute, Ind.	Terre Haute, Ind.	1904	2	72	120
Interstate Public Service Co.	Indianapolis, Ind.	Columbus, Ind.	1909	1	72	45
Int'l. Creo. & Con. Co.	Galveston, Tex.	Beaumont, Tex.	1892 1897	1	108	140
" " " "	" "	Galveston, Tex.	1905	1	72	100
" " " "	" "	Texarkana, Ark.	1902	1 1	114 72	165 125
Jennison-Wright Co.	Toledo, O.	Toledo, O.	1910	2	72	130
Kettle River Co.	Minneapolis, Minn.	Madison, Ill.	1909	4	84	135
" " "	" "	Sandstone, Minn.	1904	2	72	120
Louisiana Creosoting Co.	Winnfield, La.	Winnfield, La.	1906	1 1	72 72	126 80
L. & N. R. R. Co.	Louisville, Ky.	Guthrie, Ky.	1913	2	84	133
" " " " " "	" "	Gautier, Miss.	1895 1916	1 1 1	72 72 84	115 133 133
Michigan Pipe Co.	Bay City, Mich.	Bay City, Mich.	1893	1	72	42
Michigan Wood Preserving Co.	Pittsburgh, Pa.	Reed City, Mich.	1913	1	90	90
Mo., Kan & Tex. Ry. Co.	St. Louis, Mo.	Dennison, Tex.	1909	4	72	108
Moss Tie Co., T. J.	" " "	Mt. Vernon, Ill.	1899	1 1	74 72	132 117
Nat'l Lbr. & Creo. Co.	Texarkana, Ark.	Texarkana, Tex.	1910	2	84	132
" " " "	" "	Houston, Tex.	1912	4	72	120
Norfolk Creosoting Co.	Norfolk, Va.	Buell (nr. Norfolk),Va.	1896 1905	4 1 1	78 78 84	100 105 125
Northern Pacific Ry. Co.	St. Paul, Minn.	Brainerd, Minn.	1907	2	84	134
Ohio Wood Preserving Co.	Pittsburgh, Pa.	Orrville, O.	1912	1	84	90
Oregon-Wash. R. R. & Nav. Co.	Portland, Oregon	Wyeth, Oregon	1904	4	72	114
Pacific Creosoting Co.	Seattle, Wash.	Eagle Harbor, Wash.	1906	8	73	125
Pennsylvania R. R. Co.	Philadelphia, Pa.	Mount Union, Pa.	1910	2	72	132
" " "	" "	Greenwich, Phila., Pa.	1909	1	72	132
Phila. & Reading Ry.	Port Reading, N. J.	Port Reading, N. J.	1912	2	88	140

WOOD-PRESERVING PLANTS IN UNITED STATES—(Concluded).

Managing Company	Headquarters	Location of Plant	Year Built	No.	Diam. In.	Length Ft.
					RETORTS	
Pioneer Lbr. & Creo. Co.	Ensley, Ala.	Ensley, Ala.	1911	1	74	76
Pittsburgh Wood Preserving Co.	Pittsburgh, Pa.	Adelaide, Pa.	1911	1	84	90
Puget Sound Wd. Pres. Co.	Lowell, Wash.	Lowell, Wash.	1895	1 1 1	84 72 72	117 83 52
Republic Creosoting Co.	Indianapolis, Ind.	Mobile, Ala.	1906	2	74	130
" " "	" "	Indianapolis, Ind.	1903	1	74	130
" " "	" "	Seattle, Wash.	1916	1	74	130
" " "	Minneapolis Minn.	Minneapolis, Minn.	1905	2	74	130
St. Helens Creosoting Co.	Portland, Oregon	St. Helens, Oregon	1912	4	84	136
St. Paul & Tacoma Lbr. Co.	Tacoma, Wash.	Tacoma, Wash.	1912	1	84	130
Shreveport Creosoting Co.	Louisville, Ky.	Shreveport, La.	1910	2	84	134
Southern Creosoting Co.	Slidell, La.	Slidell, La.	1879 1902	1 2	84 72	150 100
Southern Pacific Co.	San Francisco, Cal.	Latham, Oregon	1893	2	72	117
" " "	" " "	West Oakland, Cal.	1887	1 1	72 72	108 138
" " "	" " "	Los Angeles, Cal.	1907	2	72	112
Southern Paving & Const. Co.	Chattanooga, Tenn.	Pensacola, Fla.	1912	1	72	90
Southern Wood Pres. Co.	Atlanta, Ga.	Atlanta, Ga.	1908	1	72	100
S. P. L. A. & S. L. R. R. Co.	Los Angeles, Cal.	San Pedro, Cal.	1908	2	72	117
Tenn. C. I. & R. R. Co.	Birmingham, Ala.	McAdory, Ala.	1909	1	72	65
Texas & N. O. R. R. Co.	Houston, Tex.	Houston, Tex.	1890	5	72	112
Union Pacific R. R. Co.	Omaha, Neb.	Topeka, Kan.	1909	2	73	117
" " "	" "	Laramie, Wyo.	1903	2	73	117
U. S. Wood Preserving Co.	New York, N. Y.	Buell (near Norfolk), Va.	1907	2	78	150
Western Wood Pres. Co.	Spokane, Wash.	Yardley, Wash.	1912	1	84	65
Wyckoff Pipe & Creo. Co.	New York, N. Y.	Portsmouth, Va.	1881	4	74	102
Watkins Creosoting Co.	Chicago, Ill.	Metropolis, Ill.	1913	1	74	100

CANADA.

Bruce & Co., Alex.	Glasgow, Scotland	Fort Francis, Ont.	1912	1	84	76
Canada Creosoting Co., Ltd.	Toronto, Ont.	Trenton, Ont.	1913	1	84	134
Dominion Creo. Co., Ltd.	Vancouver, B. C.	Vancouver, B. C.	1910	2	90	100
Dominion Tar & Chem. Co.	Sydney, N. S.	Sydney, N. S.	1911	1	78	85
" " " "	" "	Transcona (nr. Winnipeg), Manitoba	1912	1 3	78 78	84 135
Vancouver Creosoting Co., Ltd.	Vancouver, B. C.	North Vancouver, B. C.	1916	2	84	132

MEXICO.

No data regarding treating plants in Mexico. The Mexican Central Railroad built a plant at Aguas Calientas, Mex., in 1901 to treat railroad ties with chloride of zinc. About the year 1907 the Madero Co. built a 2-retort plant at Madera, Chihuahua, Mex., to treat railroad ties with chloride of zinc.

(Corrected to Jan. 1, 1916.)

WOOD-PRESERVING PLANTS,
UNITED STATES AND CANADA.

NON-PRESSURE PROCESSES.
UNITED STATES.

Managing Company	Headquarters	Location of Plant	Year Built	Tanks or Boilers	
				No.	Size, Ft.
Allen & Son Co., Otis	Lowell, Mass.	Lowell, Mass.	1848	2	4x 8x50
" " " " "	" "	Portsmouth, N. H.	1875	4	4x 8x50
Anaconda Copper Mg. Co.	Butte, Mont.	Butte, Mont.	1909	1	10x10x10
Barnes-Lindsey Mfg. Co.	Portland, Oregon	Portland, Oregon	....	.	....
Baxter & Jordan	Los Angeles, Cal.	Los Angeles, Cal.	1911	.	....
Carbolineum Treating & Pav. Co.	Spokane, Wash.	Spokane, Wash.	1910	1	3x 4x60
Carbolineum Wd. Pres. Co.	Portland, Oregon.	Portland, Oregon	1910	4	3x 4x60
Del. Lack. & West. R. R. Co.	Scranton, Pa.	Nanticoke, Pa.	1907	1	6 dia. x32
Homestake Mining Co.	Lead, S. D.	Lead, S. D.	1908	1	4 dia. x38
Milwaukee Ry. & Light Co.	Milwaukee, Wis.	Milwaukee, Wis.	1910	.	....
Naugle Pole & Tie Co.	Chicago, Ill.	Chicago, Ill.	1912	2	5x 5x10
Page & Hill Co.	Minneapolis, Minn.	Minneapolis, Minn.	1911	4	6 dia. x11
Pacific Light & Power Co.	Los Angeles, Cal.	Los Angeles, Cal.	1912	.	....
P. & R. Coal & Iron Co.	Pottsville, Pa.	New Philadelphia, Pa.	1908	1	6 dia. x32
Public Service Ry.	Newark, N. J.	Newark, N. J.	1909	1	10x32x 2
Puget Sound Wd. P. Co.	Lowell, Wash.	Lowell, Wash.	1895	1	3x10x30
Reeves Co., The	New Orleans, La.	New Orleans, La.	1915	1	3x 3x30
			1910	1	4x 4x30
Republic Creosoting Co.	Mobile, Ala.	Mobile, Ala.	1912	1	3x1⁹x10
San Joaquin L. & P. Co.	Fresno, Cal.	Fresno, Cal.	1910	2	7x 9x 9
" " " "	" "	San Miguel, Cal.	1910	1	7x 9x 9
St. Paul & Tacoma Lbr. Co.	Tacoma, Wash.	Tacoma, Wash.	1915	4	7x10x30
Southern Pacific Co.	San Francisco, Cal.	West Oakland, Cal.	1911	1	4x 6x 8
U. S. Govt. Wood Pres. Plant	Keokuk, Iowa	Keokuk, Iowa	1908	1	4x 3x42
" " " " "	Milan. Ill.	Milan, Ill.	1908	1	4x 3x42
" " " " "	Stillwater, Minn.	Stillwater, Minn.	1908	1	4x 3x42
" " " " "	Fountain City, Wis.	Fountain City, Wis.	1908	1	4x 3x42

CANADA.

Managing Company	Headquarters	Location of Plant	Year Built	No.	Size, Ft.
Lindsley Bros.	Spokane, Wash.	Naskup, B. C.	1910	1	6 dia. x12

(Corrected to Jan. 1, 1916.)

AMERICAN WOOD-PRESERVERS' ASSOCIATION
CONSTITUTION

(Amended 1912, 1915, 1916)

ARTICLE I.

Name and Objects.

SECTION 1. The name of this Association shall be the AMERICAN WOOD-PRESERVERS' ASSOCIATION.

SECTION 2. The objects of the Association shall be the promotion of knowledge of the materials, methods, and principles involved in the economic design, location, construction, maintenance, and operation of wood-preserving works; the standardization of specifications for wood preservatives and for their introduction into the material to be preserved; and the maintenance of high standards of business ethics in the wood-preserving industry.

SECTION 3. The means to be used for these purposes shall be meetings for the presentation and discussion of reports of the experiences and investigations of its members and others, for the interchange of ideas, and for social intercourse; the publication of desirable information; and co-operation with organizations or individuals in work affecting wood-preserving.

ARTICLE II.

Membership.

SECTION 1. The Association shall consist of Corporate, Associate, Probate, and Honorary members.

SECTION 2. A Corporate Member shall be an executive, an administrator, or an operative in a wood-preserving organization; an officer of a public-utility corporation using treated wood whose duties cover the purchasing, inspecting, treating, or distribution of such material; a chemist or an engineer in the employ of a city, county, state, nation, or public-utility corporation; a consulting chemical, civil, electrical, forest, or mechanical engineer; or a professor or an instructor in an institution of learning.

SECTION 3. An Associate Member shall be any person or association of persons interested in wood preservation or in the sale of material or equipment used in the wood-preserving industry.

SECTION 4. A Probate Member shall be an employe of a wood-preserving or inspecting organization who is not eligible for Corporate Membership.

SECTION 5. An Honorary Member shall be a person of acknowledged eminence in the wood-preserving industry or the sciences relating thereto. The number of Honorary Members shall not exceed five.

SECTION 6. Corporate Members shall have all the rights and privileges of the Association.

SECTION 7. Associate Members shall have all the rights of Corporate Members, except those of voting or holding office.

SECTION 8. Probate Members shall have all the rights of Corporate Members, except those of voting or holding office, for five years from the date of their admission, when their status shall be determined by the Executive Committee.

SECTION 9. Honorary Members shall have all the rights of Corporate Members, except that of holding office, and shall be exempt from the payment of dues.

ARTICLE III.
Admissions and Expulsions.

SECTION 1. Applications for membership and resignations from membership shall be transmitted to the Secretary-Treasurer, the former on a form prescribed by the Executive Committee and endorsed by a Corporate or an Honorary Member. The Secretary-Treasurer shall forward a copy of each application for membership to each member of the Executive Committee, the affirmative votes of a majority of whom shall admit the candidate.

SECTION 2. Proposals for Honorary Membership shall be made by at least ten members, none of whom shall be a member of the Executive Committee. The nominee shall be declared an Honorary Member if he receives the unanimous vote of the Executive Committee or the votes of two-thirds of the Corporate and Honorary members.

SECTION 3. Any member of the Association who resigns while in good standing may be reinstated without paying a second admission fee, provided his application is approved by two-thirds of the Executive Committee.

SECTION 4. For unbecoming conduct a member may be expelled by the votes of two-thirds of the members at an Annual Meeting, after the member has been served with written particulars as to his offense by the Executive Committee, and had an opportunity to be heard by it or by the members at an Annual Meeting.

SECTION 5. The Executive Committee shall accept the resignation, tendered in writing, of any member whose dues are paid.

ARTICLE IV.
Dues.

SECTION 1. On admission to the Association, members shall pay fees as follows: Corporate Members, $10.00; Associate Members, $15.00; Probate Members, $5.00, which shall include their first dues.

SECTION 2. The annual dues, payable during the first two months of the calendar year, shall be as follows: Corporate Members, $10.00; Associate Members, $10.00; Probate Members, $5.00.

SECTION 3. Members admitted after March 31 shall be exempt from the payment of dues until the following January 1, unless they desire to vote or to receive the current publications of the Association, in which case they shall pay one-half of the annual dues.

SECTION 4. Any member whose dues are unpaid on April 1 shall not receive the publications of the Association, and if his dues are not paid by December 31, his membership shall be canceled, except as provided for in Section 5 of this Article.

SECTION 5. The Executive Committee may extend the time for paying or remit the dues of any Corporate or Probate members who are unable to pay them.

ARTICLE V.

Officers.

SECTION 1. The officers of the Association shall be Corporate Members and shall consist of a President, a First Vice-President, a Second Vice-President, a Secretary-Treasurer, and six Members of Executive Committee, who, together with the last Past-President who is a Corporate Member, shall constitute the Executive Committee in which responsibility for the government of the Association shall be vested. The President shall be chosen from the nine eligible members of the Executive Committee.

SECTION 2. No two or more officers in any year shall be members of the same business organization.

SECTION 3. The President, the First Vice-President, the Second Vice-President, the Secretary-Treasurer, and two Members of Executive Committee shall be elected at each Annual Meeting.

SECTION 4. The terms of the President, Vice-Presidents, and Secretary-Treasurer shall begin at the close of the Annual Meeting at which they are elected and continue until their successors are elected and have qualified. The six Members of Executive Committee shall serve three years, two being elected each year.

SECTION 5. A vacancy in the office of President shall be filled by the Vice-Presidents in order.

SECTION 6. A vacancy in any office other than that of President shall be filled by an appointee of the Executive Committee.

SECTION 7. The President shall not be eligible for re-election to that office until three others have filled it. A Vice-President shall not be eligible for re-election to the same office until one other has filled it.

ARTICLE VI.

Nomination and Election of Officers.

SECTION 1. At each Annual Meeting six Corporate Members who are not officers shall be elected, together with the three last Past-Presidents who are Corporate Members, to serve one year as a Nominating Committee, of which the senior Past-President shall be chairman.

SECTION 2. The Nominating Committee shall nominate one eligible member for each office and for each membership in the Nominating Committee and shall send its list of nominees to the Secretary-Treasurer before October 15. Any vacancies that may occur in the list of nominees before it is sent to the members shall be filled by the Executive Committee.

SECTION 3. The voting shall not be restricted to the names presented by the Nominating Committee. Any member may file with the Secretary-Treasurer before November 1 the name of a candidate for any office.

SECTION 4. The ballot, with envelopes for secret voting, shall be sent to each member before December 1. It must contain the names of all nominees for each office, arranged alphabetically where there is more than one name for any office, with the nominees of the Nominating Committee plainly indicated.

SECTION 5. Members may scratch or substitute the name of any nominee for any office.

SECTION 6. Ballots shall be sealed and sent or delivered to the Secretary-Treasurer before the polls close, prior to which time a voter may withdraw or replace his ballot.

SECTION 7. The polls shall be closed at noon on the first day of the Annual Meeting, and the ballots shall be counted by one Corporate and four Associate or Probate Members, appointed tellers by the presiding officer at the Annual Meeting.

SECTION 8. The persons who receive the highest number of votes for the offices for which they are candidates shall be declared elected. In case of a tie between candidates for the same office, the members present at the Annual Meeting shall elect the officer from the candidates so tied. The presiding officer shall announce to the meeting the names of the officers elected.

ARTICLE VII.

Management.

SECTION 1. The President shall have general supervision of the affairs of the Association, shall preside at its meetings and those of the Executive Committee, and shall be a member ex-officio of every committee except the Nominating Committee.

SECTION 2. The Vice-Presidents, in order of seniority, shall preside at meetings in the absence of the President, and discharge his duties in case of a vacancy in the office.

SECTION 3. The Secretary-Treasurer, under the direction of the President and the Executive Committee, shall be the executive officer of the Association. He shall conduct the correspondence of the Association; record the proceedings of all meetings; collect and deposit all moneys due the Association; verify all bills and pay them when approved by the President or Executive Committee; make at each Annual Meeting a report of the accounts and membership of the Association; and perform such other duties as may be assigned to him by the Executive Committee.

SECTION 4. The Executive Committee shall manage the affairs of the Association, and shall have full power to control and regulate all matters not provided for in the Constitution. It shall act on applications for membership; make appropriations for specific purposes; direct the care of the surplus funds of the Association; and audit the accounts of the Secretary-Treasurer.

SECTION 5. The Executive Committee shall publish the activities of the Association in a book to be known as the Annual Proceedings; but, subject to the action of the Association, it may withhold, in whole or in part, discussions, papers, or reports, the propriety or soundness of which it considers questionable.

SECTION 6. The Executive Committee shall have printed a Manual of Recommended Practice, in which shall be published the specifications and standards approved by the Association in accordance with Article X.

SECTION 7. The Executive Committee shall meet at such times and places as the President may direct, or five members may request in writing. Six members shall constitute a quorum.

ARTICLE VIII.

Meetings.

SECTION 1. An Annual Meeting, at which the officers shall be elected and all annual reports read, shall be held on the fourth Tuesday in January of each year, at ten o'clock A. M., at such place as the Association at the previous meeting may designate.

SECTION 2. Whenever the President may deem it necessary, or upon the written application of fifteen Corporate Members, he shall direct the Secretary-Treasurer to call a special meeting. The call for such a meeting shall state the time, place, and purpose of the meeting, and shall be mailed not less than thirty days prior to the date of the proposed meeting.

SECTION 3. Twenty Corporate Members shall constitute a quorum at any meeting of the Association.

SECTION 4. The order of business at the meetings of the Association shall be arranged by the Executive Committee, subject to addition or change by the votes of the majority of the members present.

ARTICLE IX.
Amendments.

SECTION 1. Proposed amendments to this Constitution must be offered in writing, signed by at least five Corporate Members, and forwarded to the Secretary-Treasurer not less than thirty days prior to the Annual Meeting. They shall be published with the notices for the meeting.

SECTION 2. Proposed amendments shall be in order for discussion at the Annual Meeting, and may be amended and adopted if two-thirds of the votes of the Corporate and Honorary members present and voting are affirmative.

ARTICLE X.
Adoption of Standards.

SECTION 1. Any proposals for the approval or recommendation by the Association, of definitions, methods, nomenclature, specifications, standard construction, or standard practice, or aimed at defining formally the position of the Association on any matter of importance, shall be presented in writing, with drawings if necessary, at an Annual Meeting. At this meeting amendments may be made by a majority of the Corporate and Honorary members present and voting. Proposed standards shall be referred to letter ballot of the Association if two-thirds of the Corporate and Honorary members at an Annual Meeting vote affirmatively. The affirmative votes of two-thirds of all the Corporate and Honorary members shall be required for the adoption of any standard.

AMERICAN WOOD-PRESERVERS' ASSOCIATION
OFFICERS AND COMMITTEES

OFFICERS FOR 1916.

Carl G. Crawford..President
John Foley..First Vice-President
M. K. Trumbull..Second Vice-President
F. J. Angier...............Secretary-Treasurer, Mt. Royal Station, Baltimore, Md.

EXECUTIVE COMMITTEE.

Carl G. Crawford, *Chairman*

Angier, F. J.	Davidson, G. M. } Term, 2 Years	
Foley, John	Rex, Geo. E. }	
Trumbull, M. K.	Card, J. B. }	
Joyce, A. R. } Term, 3 Years	Hendricks, V. K. } Term, 1 Year	
Pooler, F. S. }	Waterman, J. H. }	

STANDING COMMITTEES FOR 1916.

No. 1—Preservatives.

E. B. Fulks, *Chairman*

Acree, S. F.   Fulweiler, W. H.   Steinmayer, O. C.
Church, S. R.   Kammerer, A, L.   Taylor, C. M.
Forrest, C. N.   Larkin, A. E.

No. 2—Specifications for the Purchase and Preservation of Treatable Timber

A. R. Joyce, *Chairman*

Card, J. B.   Martin, F. R.   Smith, Lowry
Goss, O P. M.   Rex, Geo. E.   Sterling, E. A.
                    Winslow, C. P.

No. 3—Wood Block Paving.

C. H. Teesdale, *Chairman*

Buehler, Walter   Hamilton, F. P.   Newton, H. M.
Cherrington, F. W. Loud, H. S.

No. 4—Plant Operation.

A. L. Kuehn, *Chairman*

Hunt, Geo. M.   Lockett, A. M.   Meyer, August
Lane, C. W.   McArdle, Frank

No. 5—Service Tests of Ties and Structural Timber.

C. P. Winslow, *Chairman*

Bowser, E. H.   Gosline, C. E.   Rollins, H. M.
Ford, C. F.   Mattos, F. D.   von Schrenk, Hermann

No. 6—Service Tests of Wood Block Paving.

L. B. Moses, *Chairman*

Calder, R. J.   Dutton, F. R.   Williams, J. C.
Dow, Allan W.   Manley, R. S.   Winslow, Geoffrey
Draper, E. G.   Smith, Phil R.

SPECIAL COMMITTEES FOR 1916.

Publicity, Promotion and Education.

E. A. Sterling, *Chairman*

Bates, John S.   Howson, E. T.   Schnatterbeck, C. C.
Brown, Nelson C.   Record, Samuel J.   Swan, O. T.
Hamilton, F. P.   Ridsdale, P. S.

Terminology.

J. B. Card, *Chairman*

Howson, E. T.   Hunt, Geo. M.   Shipley, G. B.
                    Trumbull, M. K.

Program.

John Foley, *Chairman*

Davidson, G. M.   Hendricks, V. K.   Joyce, A. R.
                    Trumbull, M. K.

Entertainment.

Jesse I. Eppinger, *Chairman*

Draper, E. G.   Loud, H. S.   Williams, J. C.
Lembcke, G. A.   Shipley, L. B.

AMERICAN WOOD-PRESERVERS' ASSOCIATION
MEMBERS

c-Corporate. a-Associate. p-Probate. h-Honorary.
Figures indicate serial number of Membership Certificates.

324 c ACREE, S. F.............In Charge Section of Derived Products, Forest Product Laboratory, Madison Wis.

183 c ALEXANDER, E. E......General Foreman, Timber Preserving Plant, Baltimore and Ohio R. R. Co., Green Spring, W. Va.

29 c ALLARDYCE, R. L.......Supt., International Creosoting & Construction Co., Texarkana, Tex.

21 c ALLERTON, DAVID......Carlotta, Cal.

1 c ANGIER, F. J...........Supt. of Timber Preservation, Baltimore and Ohio R. R. Co., Baltimore, Md.

274 c APPEL, HARRIS A.......Engineer, Bruno Grosche & Co., 90 Wall Street, N. Y.

2 c ARMSTRONG, R. L.......636 Burdette St., New Orleans, La.

105 c BACON, W. L............Supt. Tie Treating Plant, C. & N. W. Ry., Escanaba, Mich.

225 c BAKER, HUGH P.......Dean, New York State College of Forestry, Syracuse, N. Y.

3 h BAKER, J. S............Box 22, Paducah, Ky.

167 c BATEMAN, ERNEST.....Chemist, Forest Products Laboratory, Madison, Wis.

246 c BATES, JOHN S.........Supt., Forest Products Laboratories, McGill University, Montreal, Canada.

88 c BATSON, C. D...........Manager, Republic Creosoting Co., Mobile, Ala.

4 c BEAL, F. D.............Sales Engineer, Chas. R. McCormick & Co., 800 Fife Bldg., San Francisco, Cal.

255 c BEATY, R. ERNEST......Expert on Wood Preservation, 30 Church St., New York.

198 c BECKER, A. C...........Chief Tie & Timber Inspector, Grand Trunk Ry., Montreal, Canada.

295 a BELANGER, ERNEST....Consulting Engineer, Elder Ebano Asphalt Co., 364 University St., Montreal, Canada.

145 c BELCHER, R. S.........Supt. Treating Plant, Santa Fe Tie & Lumber Pres. Co., Somerville, Tex.

144 c BERK, P. F..............Chemical Mfr., F. W. Berk & Co., Ltd., 1 Fenchurch Ave. London, England.

5 h BERRY, C. W...........Consulting Engineer, care of J. B. Berry, Transportation Bldg., Chicago, Ill.

300 c BLACK, JAMES M.......Paving Block Expert, 203 Pasadena Apts., Jefferson & Du Bois Sts., Detroit, Mich.

22 c BOEHNE, E. E..........Office Manager, International Creosoting & Construction Co., Galveston, Tex.

258 c BOOK, J. E..............Treating Engineer, Pacific Creosoting Co., Creosote, Wash.

244 c BOWSER, E. H..........Supt. of Timber Department, I. C. R. R., Memphis, Tenn.

267 a BOYD, J. L..............Chief Engineer Creosoted Block Paving Co., Royal Bank Bldg., Toronto, Canada.

280 p BRENNAN, T. S.........Lumber Inspector, A., T. & S. F. Ry., Box 503, Ballard Station, Seattle, Wash.

301 c BRIGHT, EDGAR W......Tie & Timber Agent, Boston Elevated Rwy. Co., 101 Milk St., Boston, Mass.

340 c BROWN, F. I............ Lumber Agent, Pennsylvania Lines West, Fort Wayne, Ind.

230 c BROWN, NELSON C.....Professor of Forest Utilization, New York State College of Forestry, Syracuse, N. Y.

122 c BRUNING, HEINRICH...(Robert A. Munro & Co., 31 Liberty St., New York City) Hubertusmuhle, Schopfurth, Mark, Germany.

23 c BUEHLER, WALTER.....Consulting Engineer on Wood Preservation, The Barrett Co., 10 S. La Salle St., Chicago, Ill.

24 c BURKHALTER, D........American Creosoting Co., Box 77, Russell, Ky.

338 c BURY, RICHARD A......Asst. Gen. Tie Agent, New York Central Lines, 76 Seward Ave., Detroit, Mich.

83 a CABOT, SAMUEL........Mfg. Chemist, 141 Milk St., Boston, Mass.

30 c CALDER, R. J...........Secy.-Treas., International Creosoting & Construction Co., Galveston, Tex.

190 c   CAMPBELL, J. H.........Chief Chemist, R. W. Hunt & Co., 2200 Insurance Exchange, Chicago, Ill.
43 c   CARD, J. B..............Manager, Chicago Creosoting Co., 30 N. LaSalle St., Chicago, Ill.
276 c   CECIL, WM. A...........Wood-Preserving Engineer, Indiana Tie Co., Citizens National Bank Building, Evansville, Ind.
257 c   CHADBOURNE, B........Asst. Supt., Pacific Creosoting Co., Creosote, Wash.
302 c   CHAPIN, E. T...........Prest., The E. T. Chapin Co., 2008 Railway Exchange Bldg., St. Louis, Mo.
69 c   CHERRINGTON, F. W....Chief Engr., Jennison-Wright Co., 313 Huron St., Toledo. O.
19 c   CHRISTIAN, EDMUND...Gen. Mgr., Norfolk Creosoting Co., Norfolk, Va.
57 a   CHURCH, SUMNER R....Manager, Research Dept., The Barrett Co., 17 Battery Place, New York.
165 c   CLARKE, G. S...........Vice-Prest. & Gen. Mgr., The Reeves Co., 809 Whitney-Central Bldg., New Orleans, La.
184 c   CLARK, W. DENNISON..Vice-Prest. & Gen. Mgr., Columbia Creosoting Co., 810 Lewis Bldg., Portland, Ore.
318 c   CLEMENTS, A. B.......Vice-Prest., United States Wood Preserving Co., 165 Broadway, New York.
319 p   CLEMENTS, CYRIL M..Sales Engineer, The Barrett Co., Philadelphia, Pa.
174 c   CLIFTON, W. H.........Lumber Agent, Baltimore & Ohio R. R. Co., Baltimore, Md.
249 c   COBEAN, CHAS. E.......Supt., Pacific Creosoting Co., Creosote, Wash.
188 a   COCKE, W. H...........Prest., Commercial Acid Co., 3943 Duncan Ave., St. Louis, Mo.
157 c   COLLIER, H. L..........Chief of Construction, City of Atlanta, Ga.
218 c   COLLIVER, S. R.........Treatment Inspector, A., T. & S. F. Ry., Topeka, Kan.
67 c   COLMAN, GEO. A.......The J. M. Colman Co., Colman Bldg., Seattle, Wash.
221 c   COOPER, S. D...........Chief Inspector, A., T. & S. F. Ry., Topeka, Kan.
31 c   CRAWFORD, CARL G....Gen. Mgr., American Creosoting Co., 808 Columbia Bldg., Louisville, Ky.
80 c   CURTIS, W. W..........Prest. & Treas., The Rapson Coal Mining Co., Box 485, Colorado Springs, Colo.

25 c   DAVIDSON, G. M........Chemist & Engineer of Tests, C. & N. W. Ry. Co., Chicago, Ill.
143 c   DAVIES, E. T...........Inspector, City Engineer's Office, Minneapolis, Minn.
84 c   DE CEW, J. A...........Chemical Engineer, McGill Bldg., Montreal, Canada.
272 c   DELIUS, E. A...........Bookkeeper, Pacific Creosoting Co., Seattle, Wash.
204 c   DEMUTH, R. E..........Testing Engineer, 22 Hayward Ave., Baltimore, Md.
223 c   DIXON, G. C............Tie Treating Inspector, N. Y. C. Lines, Box 763, Indianapolis, Ind.
64 c   DIXON, J. H............Forestry Branch, Dept. Natural Resources, Canadian Pac. Ry., Calgary, Alberta, Canada.
119 c   DOUGHERTY, CURTIS...Chief Engineer, Queen & Crescent R. R., Cincinnati, O.
303 c   DOVEY, J. THOMAS.....Prest., The Seattle Engineering Co., 724 Central Building, Seattle, Wash.
290 c   DOW, ALLAN W........Consulting Engineer, Dow & Smith, 131 E. 23rd St., N. Y.
121 c   DRAPER, E. G..........Prest., American Creosoting Co. of N. J., 17 Battery Place, New York.
166 a   DREFAHL, LOUIS C.....Chemist, Grasselli Chemical Co., 880 The Arcade, Cleveland, Ohio.
93 c   DRINKER, W. W........Asst. Engineer, Erie R. R. Co., 50 Church St., New York.
178 c   DUNSTAN, J. H.........Supt., Southern Creosoting Co., Slidell, La.
211 c   DURHAM, J. H..........Vice-Prest., American Creosoting Co., Louisville, Ky.
322 c   DUTTON, ELLIS R.......Asst. City Engr., City Hall, Minneapolis, Minn.

202 a   EASTWICK, CHAS. H....Prest., The Northeastern Co., 6 Beacon St., Boston, Mass.
297 a   ELLIOTT, J. A...........Tie & Timber Contractor, 1609 Mound Ave., Jacksonville, Ill.
275 c   EMERSON,HARRINGTONPrest., The Emerson Co., 30 Church St., New York.
76 c   EPPINGER, JESSE I.....Gen. Mgr., Eppinger & Russell Co., 165 Broadway, New York.
163 c   ERICSON, L. T..........Engineer, American Creosoting Co. of N. J., 17 Battery Place, New York.

158 c   FANT, A. E.............Gen. Mgr., Gulfport Creosoting Co., Gulfport, Miss.

9 h FAULKNER, E. O.......Mgr., Tie & Timber Dept., A., T. & S. F. Ry., Kerckhoff
        Bldg., Los Angeles, Cal.
159 a FENN, FRANK D........Mgr., Railroad Sales Dept., The Crane Co., Chicago, Ill.
239 c FERGUSSON, HUBERT..Gen. Mgr., Burt, Boulton & Haywood, Ltd., Prince Regent's
        Wharf, Silverton, Victoria Docks, London, England.
237 c FINKE, W. F. H.........Tie & Timber Agent, Southern Ry. Co., Washington, D. C.
62 c FISHER, WM. A.........Lembcke, von Bernuth Co., 171 Madison Ave., New York.
308 a FOERSTERLING, DR. H..Vice-Prest., Roessler & Hasslacher Chemical Co.,
        380 High St., Perth Amboy, N. J.
77 c FOLEY, JOHN...........Forester, P. R. R. Co., Broad St. Station, Philadelphia, Pa.
106 c FORD, C. F............Supt. Tie and Timber Dept., C., R. I. & P. R. R.,
        325 LaSalle St. Sta., Chicago, Ill.
296 c FORREST, CHAS. N......Chief Chemist, Barber Asphalt Paving Co., Maurer, N. J.
313 c FOWLER, J. W..........Asst. Efficiency Engineer, Baltimore & Ohio R. R. Co.,
        Baltimore, Md.
117 c FREY, GEO. W..........Secy.-Treas. & Mgr., Compressed Wood Preserving Co.,
        4600 Spring Grove Ave., Cincinnati, O.
333 c FRISTOE, J. W.........Prest., T. J. Moss Tie Co., Security Bldg., St. Louis, Mo.
38 c FULKS, E. B............Vice-Prest., American Tar Products Co., 208 S. LaSalle St.,
        Chicago, Ill.
160 a FULWEILER, W. H......Chemist, United Gas Improvement Co., 1706 N. Broad St.,
        Philadelphia, Pa.
306 a FURLONG, L. A.........Vice-Prest., The Valentine-Clark Co., Security Bldg.,
        Minneapolis, Minn.

44 a GERHARD, H. H........Prest., C-A Wood-Preserver Co., 807 Wright Bldg.,
        St. Louis, Mo.
39 c GIBSON, ANDREW......Engineer Maintenance of Way, No. Pac. Ry., St. Paul, Minn.
161 a GIBSON, LOUIS S.......Secy., Sandoval Zinc Co., 410 N. Peoria St., Chicago, Ill.
180 a GIBSON, W. C..........Sales Engineer, Allis-Chalmers Mfg. Co., Milwaukee, Wis.
316 p GOLDSTEIN, H. I.......Highway Inspector, Bureau of Highways, Dept. of Public
        Works, 4200 Woodland Ave., Philadelphia, Pa.
56 c GOLTRA, W. F..........Prest., W. F. Goltra Tie Co., Rockefeller Bldg., Cleveland, O.
288 c GOSLINE, C. E.........Treating Inspector, D., L. & W. R. R. Co., Paterson, N. J.
277 c GOSS, O. P. M..........Consulting Timber Engineer, Seattle, Wash.
243 c GRADY, W. H..........Asst. Gen. Supt., American Creosoting Co., Louisville, Ky.
100 c GRAHAM, FLOYD N....Timber Inspector, C. G. W. R. R. Chicago, Ill.
170 c GREEN, DONALD W.....Secy., Columbia Creosoting Co., 809 Lewis Bldg., Portland,
        Ore.
232 c GRIFFIN, RUSSELL A...Mgr. Pole Dept., Western Electric Co., 463 West St.,
        New York.
334 c GRIGGS, E. G..........Prest., St. Paul & Tacoma Lumber Co., Tacoma, Wash.
321 c GRIMES, I. B..........Plant Supt., National Lumber & Creosoting Co., Houston, Tex.
72 a GROW, J. H............Sales Engineer, Allis-Chalmers Mfg. Co., Milwaukee, Wis.

231 c HAGGANDER, G. A......Asst. Bridge Engineer, C., B. & Q. R. R. Co., 547 W.
        Jackson Blvd., Chicago, Ill.
220 c HALL, CHAS. S.........Supt. of Construction, P. O. Box 137, Brunswick, Ga.
195 c HAMILTON, F. P........Paving Engineer, Southern Pine Association, 601 Interstate
        Bank Bldg., New Orleans, La.
214 c HAMNETT, W. S.........Vice-Prest. & Mgr., Pittsburgh Testing Laboratory of Texas,
        305 Praetorian Bldg., Dallas, Tex.
213 c HARDEN, G. S..........Supt. Timber Preserving Plant, B., R. & P. Ry., Bradford, Pa.
187 c HARRIS, PAGE..........Vice-Prest., National Lumber & Creosoting Co., Houston, Tex.
123 a HARTLEY, C. H.........Gen. Mgr., Wisconsin & Northern R. R. Co., Oshkosh, Wis.
82 c HARTMAN, E. F........Prest., Carbolineum Wood Preserving Co., 182 Franklin St.,
        New York.
53 a HAWKES, A. W.........Sales Manager, General Chemical Co., 112 W. Adams St.,
        Chicago, Ill.
236 c HELSON, J. R...........Supt., Watkins Creosoting Co., Metropolis, Ill.
103 c HENDRICKS, V. K.......Asst. Chief Engineer, St. Louis & San Francisco Ry. Co.,
        Frisco Bldg., St. Louis, Mo.
335 c HERMANN, GEO. E......Mgr., Vancouver Creosoting Co., Standard Bank Bldg., Van-
        couver, British Columbia.

212 c HERT, A. T..............Prest., American Creosoting Co., Louisville, Ky.
75 c HESS, LAWRENCE E....Asst. Supt., Republic Creosoting Co., Indianapolis, Ind.
294 c HIGGINS, CHAS. C......Care of J. W. Kendrick, 14 E. Jackson Blvd., Chicago, Ill.
320 c HILL, L. L..............Secretary, The Page & Hill Co., Plymouth, Bldg., Minneapolis, Minn.
179 c HORROCKS, H. E........Mgr., Pacific Creosoting Co., Seattle, Wash.
193 c HOWSON, E. T..........Engineering Editor, "Railway Age Gazette," Transportation Bldg., Chicago, Ill.
342 c HOYT, HERBERT B.....Asst. Supt. Timber Preserving Plant, B. R. & P. Rwy., Bradford, Pa.
265 c HUNT, GEO. M..........Chemist, Forest Products Laboratory, Madison, Wis.
224 c IKIN, A. J................Cost Statement Engineer, Southern Pac. Co., Box 6, Kern, Cal.
299 p IRVING, A. E...........Clerk, Tie Plant, Baltimore & Ohio R. R. Co., Green Spring, W. Va.
252 c JACKSON, W. E.........Supt., Treating Plant, Santa Fe Tie & Lbr. Pres. Co., Albuquerque, N. M.
124 c JENNISON, H. G........Prest., Jennison-Wright Co., 313 Huron St., Toledo, O.
260 c JOHNSON, J. A..........Foreman, Tie Preserving Plant, U. P. R. R. Co., Box 303, Laramie, Wyo.
136 a JOHNSON, J. H..........B. Johnson & Son, Richmond, Ind.
66 c JOYCE, A. R.............Joyce-Watkins Co., 332 S. Michigan Ave., Chicago, Ill.
147 c JUDGE, F. B.............Supt. Timber Preservation, C. H. & N. Ry., Hull, Fla.
205 c KAMMERER, A. L........Consulting Engineer, von Schrenk & Kammerer, Tower Grove & Fladd Aves., St. Louis, Mo.
222 c KEIG, J. R..............Treatment Inspector, A., T. & S. F. Ry. Co., Topeka, Kan.
292 c KELLOGG, R. S.........Secy., National Lumber Mfrs. Assn., 925 Lumber Exchange, Chicago, Ill.
315 h KENDRICK, J. W........Consulting Engineer, 14 E. Jackson Blvd., Chicago, Ill.
281 c KENT, A. S.............Ch. Engr., Monon Route, C., I. & L. Ry. Co., Transportation Bldg., Chicago, Ill.
201 c KROEMER, F. W........Chemist, Santa Fe Tie & Lbr. Pres. Co., Somerville, Tex.
60 c KUCKUCK, BERTHOLD..Representing Hulsberg & Co., 1357 E. 48th St., Chicago, Ill.
162 c KUEHN, A. L............Gen. Supt., American Tar Products Co., 208 S. LaSalle St., Chicago, Ill.
266 c KYNOCK, WM..........Assistant in Wood Preservation, Forest Products Laboratories of Canada, McGill University, Montreal, Can.
20 c LABROT, S. W..........Prest., American Creosote Works, New Orleans, La.
282 c LA GRONE, J. M.........Mgr., Louisiana Creosoting Co., Winnfield, La.
208 c LANE, CHAS. E.........Supt. Creosoting Plant, St. Paul & Tacoma Lumber Co., Tacoma, Wash.
153 c LANE, C. W..............Supervisor Timber Preserving Plants, Baltimore & Ohio R. R. Co., Green Spring, W. Va.
229 a LANGE, ALBERT.........European Manager, Lembcke, von Bernuth Co., 4 Lloyds Ave., London, E. C., England.
332 c LANGE, L. H.............Secy., Northern Timber Products Co., Security Lumber Bldg., Minneapolis, Minn.
59 c LARKIN, A. E............Mgr., Republic Creosoting Co., Plymouth Bldg., Minneapolis, Minn.
317 a LATTIMORE, C. H.......Prest., Creosoted Block Paving Co., Royal Bank Bldg., Toronto, Canada.
96 c LAWSON, W. W.........Supt. Wood-Preserving Works, T. & N. O. Ry. Co., Houston, Tex.
328 a LEE, ROBERT E.........Vice-Prest., Hobart Lee Tie Co., Springfield, Mo.
40 a LEMBCKE, G. A..........Lembcke, von Bernuth Co., 171 Madison Ave., New York.
110 c LEWIS, F. J.............Prest., F. J. Lewis Mfg. Co., 2500 S. Robey St., Chicago, Ill.
118 c LEWIS, WM. H..........Vice-Prest., F. J. Lewis Mfg. Co., 2500 S. Robey St., Chicago, Ill.
148 c LINDLEY, S. B..........Engineer, Western Wood-Preserving Co., 611 Peyton Bldg., Spokane, Wash.
215 c LINDSEY, JOHN B., Jr...Supt. Timber Treating Plant, L. & N. R. R. Co., Gautier, Miss.
199 a LOCKETT, A. M.........Prest., A. M. Lockett & Co., 533 Baronne St., New Orleans, La.

12 c LOGAN, JOHN T.........Prest., National Lumber & Creosoting Co., Texarkana, Ark.

242 c LOOK, RICHARD V......Prest., Canada Creosoting Co., Ltd., 1 King St., E., Toronto, Canada.

112 c LORD, RUSSELL.........Ayer & Lord Tie Co., Railway Exchange, Chicago, Ill.

61 c LOUD, H. S.............Vice-President, Railway Tie Treating Co., 165 Broadway, N. Y.

73 a LOUNSBURY, JAS. A....Vice-Prest., Greenlee Bros. & Co., Rockford, Ill.

151 a LUND, C. A.............Mgr., C. A. Lund Co., Merriam Park P. O., St. Paul, Minn.

196 c MAITLAND, G. F........Division Engineer, Union Pacific R. R. Co., Kansas City, Mo.

41 c MANLEY, R. S.........Prest., Creosoted Wood Block Paving Co., Queen & Crescent Bldg., New Orleans, La.

p MANION, KERON.......Asst. Supt., American Creosoting Co., Newark, N. J.

263 c MARRIOTT, F. G........Engineer of Tests, Department of Works, Foot of Princess St., Toronto, Can.

336 a MARTIN, JAS. R........Vice-Prest., Western Silo Co., Des Moines, Iowa.

329 p MARTIN, LYMAN C......Clerk, American Creosoting Co., Indianapolis, Ind.

250 c MARTIN, F. R...........Treating Inspector, C. & E. I. R. R. Co., Box 856, Marion, Ill.

137 c MATTOS, F. D..........Supt., Creosoting Works, Southern Pacific Co., West Oakland, Cal.

52 c McARDLE, FRANK.......Supt. Tie Plant, Indiana Zinc Creosoting Co., Terre Haute, Ind.

279 c McCANDLESS, S. F.....Mgr. Tie Dept., Canada Creosoting Co., 1 King St. E., Toronto, Can.

113 c MEREDITH, W. C.......Supt., Southern Wood-Preserving Co., Atlanta, Ga.

71 c MEYER, AUGUST........Supervisor Tie Plant, C., B. & Q. R. R. Co., Galesburg, Ill.

70 a MILLS, W. C............Salesman, Grasselli Chemical Co., The Arcade, Cleveland, O.

185 c MIMS, L...............Fuel & Timber Agent, Southern Pacific Co., Houston, Tex.

32 a MITCHELL, L. E........Prest., Dallas, Corsicana & Palestine Ry., Palestine, Tex.

164 c MOLL, DR. FRIEDRICH..4 Brandenburgische St., Sudende, Berlin, Germany.

254 c MOORE, ROBERT H.....Chief Engineer, American Creosoting Co., Louisville, Ky.

114 c MOSES, L. B...........Sales Manager, The Kettle River Co., Plymouth Bldg., Minneapolis, Minn.

309 c MURCHIE, WILFRED E..Consulting Inspector, Shillito & Murchie, Maritime Exchange Bldg., New York.

240 c MURRAY, D. L.........Gen. Foreman, Tie Plant, Santa Fe Tie & Lbr. Pres. Co., Somerville, Tex.

307 p MYERLY, J. R..........Treating Engr. Timber Preserving Plant, Baltimore & Ohio R. R. Co., Green Spring, W. Va.

50 c NEWTON, H. M.........Manager of Plants, The Kettle River Co., Plymouth Bldg., Minneapolis, Minn.

283 a NIXON, E. A............Vice-Prest., Western Tie & Timber Co., 905 Syndicate Trust Bldg., St. Louis, Mo.

314 a NIXON, WARREN C.....Secy., Western Tie & Timber Co., 905 Syndicate Trust Bldg., St. Louis, Mo.

186 c NOYES, A. H...........Secy.-Treas., Ayer & Lord Tie Co., 1515 Railway Exchange, Chicago, Ill.

146 c NOYES, GEO. W........Supt., Timber Treating Plant, M., K. & T. Lines, Denison, Tex.

33 a OKES, DAY.............Contractor & Engineer, Hanlon & Okes, 319 Lumber Exchange, Minneapolis, Minn.

337 c ORUMM, EDMUND O....Chief Inspector, Seattle Port Commission, Avalon Apartments, Seattle, Wash.

273 c PADDOCK, EDW. F......Chem. Engr., Carbolineum Wood Pres. Co., 182 Franklin St., New York.

253 c PARK, ERNEST S.......Sales Engineer, The Rodd Co., 1402 Commonwealth Bldg., Pittsburgh, Pa.

26 c PARMINTER, L. I........Sales Agent, Long Bell Lumber Co., Long Bldg., Kansas City, Mo.

268 c PARROTT, R. D.........Prest. & Gen. Mgr., Atlantic Creosoting & Wood Preserving Works, Norfolk, Va.

271 c PAUL, H. A.............Treating Inspr., C., R. I. & P. and M. P. Ry., Tie Plant, Ark.

343 c PEARSON, R. S.........Forest Economist, Forest Research Institute, Dehra Dun, U. P. India.

227 c PERRY, ARTHUR W.....Night Gen. Foreman, Santa Fe Tie & Lbr. Pres. Co., Somerville, Tex.
191 c PESTEL, A. C...........Supt. Tie Treating Plant, O., W. R. R. & N. Co., Wyeth, Ore.
217 c PINSON, J. F...........Asst. Engineer Bridge & Buildings, C. M. & St. P. Ry., Seattle, Wash.
142 c POLLOCK, SAMUEL T...Asst. Supt. Tie Plant, Atlantic Coast Line, Gainesville, Fla.
115 c POOLER, F. S...........Tie Agent, C. M. & St. P. Ry., 1352 Railway Exchange, Chicago, Ill.
182 c POWELL, A. O., Jr......Chemical Engineer, 404 Central Bldg., Seattle, Wash.
91 c POWELL, E. L...........Prest., New Orleans-Cuban Steamship Co., 802 Canal Bank Bldg., New Orleans, La.

284 c QUINCY, R. B...........Representing R. W. Hunt & Co., 1022 Hibernian Bldg., New Orleans, La.

261 c RAWSON, R. H..........Supt. of Plant, St. Helens Creosoting Co., St. Helens, Ore.
331 c RAY, JOHN R...........Inspector in Charge Gulf States Lumber Inspection, Public Service Commission of N. Y., New Orleans, La.
155 c RECORD, S. J...........Asst. Prof., Forest School, Yale University, New Haven, Conn.
226 c REDMAN, KENNETH.....Chemist, Pacific Creosoting Co., Creosote, Wash.
325 a REID, JOS. S...........Secy. & Treas., Clark Bros. Co., Olean, N. Y.
54 c REX, GEORGE E........Manager Treating Plants, A., T. & S. F. Ry., Topeka, Kan.
228 a RIDSDALE, P. S........Secy., American Forestry Ass'n, 1410 H St., N. W., Washington, D. C.
131 c ROBERTS, G. G........1 Clarges St., Piccadilly W., London, England.
278 p ROBINSON, DONALD....Student in Chemistry, 6538 Norman Blvd., Chicago, Ill.
133 c RODD, THOS., Jr......1402 Commonwealth Bldg., Pittsburgh, Pa.
264 c ROE, GEORGE J.........Asst. Treating Engineer, Pacific Creosoting Co., Creosote, Wash.
14 c ROLLINS, H. M.........Supt., Gulfport Creosoting Co., Gulfport, Miss.
311 c ROTH, E. J.............Purchasing Agent, C. I. & L. Ry., 608 S. Dearborn St., Chicago, Ill.
310 c ROWLAND, J. W........General Tie Inspector, Baltimore & Ohio R. R. Co., Baltimore, Md.
241 a RUEPING, MAX.........Owner, Hulsberg & Co., Lessingstra, Berlin, Germany.
90 c RUFLI, H. M............Supt., Republic Creosoting Co., Indianapolis, Ind.
78 c RYAN, W. J.............Supt., National Lumber & Creosoting Co., Texarkana, Ark.

286 c SACKETT, H. S..........Nat'l Lbr. Mfr's Assoc., 925 Lumber Exchange, Chicago, Ill.
330 c SAPOJNIKOFF, SERGE...Engineer-Chemist, Principal Asst. to Chief of Wood-Preserving Laboratory of Russian Ministry of Railways, Petrograd, Russia.
63 c SCHILLING, FRANK.....Supt., Eppinger & Russell Co., Long Island City, N. Y.
126 a SCHMOOK, KARL........Representing Guido Rutgers Kammandit Co., 20 Liechtensteinstrasse, Vienna, Austria.
206 c SCHNATTERBECK, C. C. Editor, "Wood-Preserving," Mt. Royal Station, Baltimore, Md.
101 c SCHOLTZ, A. C..........Supt., T. J. Moss Tie Co., Mt. Vernon, Ill.
189 c SCHOMBURG, T. A.......Prest., Continental Tie & Lumber Co., Denver, Colo.
85 c SCHULZ, HARRY........Supt. Wood-Preserving Plant, San Pedro, Los Angeles & Salt Lake R. R., Los Angeles, Cal.
233 c SEGALL, S..............Gen. Mgr., Rutgers Works, Lessingstra, Berlin, Germany.
210 c SEXTON, C. H..........Supervising Inspector, Western Electric Co., 463 West St., New York.
51 c SHIPLEY, GRANT B.....Prest., Pittsburgh Wood Preserving Co., Commonwealth Bldg., Pittsburgh, Pa.
154 a SHIPLEY, L. B.........Chemist, The Barrett Co., 17 Battery Place, New York.
89 c SHUFORD, C. S.........Supt., Republic Creosoting Co., Mobile, Ala.
98 c SIGNOR, GEO. W........Prest., Geo. W. Signor Tie Co., Shreveport, La.
262 a SJODAHL, H. A.........Chemist, Chatfield Mfg. Co., Station P, Cincinnati, O.
15 c SMITH, AMOS M........Supt., Ayer & Lord Tie Co., Argenta, Ark.
203 c SMITH, E. BERNARD....Gen. Mgr., Dominion Tar & Chemical Co., Transcona, Manitoba, Canada.

291 c SMITH, FRANCIS P......Consulting Engineer, Dow & Smith, 131 E. 23rd St., New
                                York.
 45 c SMITH, LOWRY.........Supt. Tie Plant, Northern Pacific R. R. Co., Brainerd, Minn.
 34 c SMITH, P. A...........Asst. Mgr., Norfolk Creosoting Co., Norfolk, Va.
 28 c SMITH, PHIL R.........5426 Sheridan Road, Chicago, Ill.
289 a SMITH, R. G...........Engineer & Chemist, Standard Oil Co., 200 Bush St., San
                                Francisco, Cal.
216 c SMITH, V. C...........Consulting Engineer, Government Railroads of India, care of
                                Parr's Bank, Ltd., London, N. W., England.
135 c SMITH, W. J...........Treating Inspector, Pittsburgh & Lake Erie R. R. Co.,
                                Adelaide, Pa.
248 c STAHL, K. F...........Consulting Chemist, General Chemical Co., 57th St. and A.
                                V. Ry., Pittsburgh, Pa.
323 c STAMFORD, A...........Supt., U. S. Wood Preserving Co., Buell, Va.
327 c STEARNS, R. B.........Vice-Prest., Milwaukee Electric Railway & Light Co., Public
                                Service Bldg., Milwaukee, Wis.
104 c STEINMAYER, O. C......General Treating Inspector, Frisco Lines, Springfield, Mo.
 58 c STERLING, E. A........Mgr., Trade Extension Dept., Nat'l Lumber Mfr's Assoc.,
                                925 Lumber Exchange, Chicago, Ill.
238 a STERNBERG, DR. LEO...Manager, Hulsberg & Co., Lessingstra, Berlin, Germany.
 13 c STEWART, F. H.........Supt. Creosoting Plant, Central of Georgia Ry., Crump's
                                Park, Ga.
 92 c STIMSON, EARL.........Engineer Maintenance of Way, Baltimore & Ohio R. R. Co.,
                                Baltimore, Md.
285 c STOCKING, E. J........Sales Manager., Chicago Creosoting Co., Chicago, Ill.
312 c STULL, T. G...........Chief Lumber Inspector, C. I. & L. R. R., Bloomington, Ind.
287 c SWAN, O. T............Sec'y, Northern Hemlock & Hardwood Mfr's Assoc., Oshkosh,
                                Wis.
129 a SWINK, ROBERT B......Gen. Mgr., Southern Tie & Lumber Co., Medon, Tenn.

 36 c TAYLOR, C. MARSHALL.Supt., Port Reading Creosoting Plant, Port Reading, N. J.
304 c TAYLOR, THOS. B.......Asst. to Prest., American Creosoting Co., Louisville, Ky.
172 c TEESDALE, CLYDE H...Asst. Engineer, Forest Products Laboratory, Madison, Wis.
 94 a TESHIMA, TOMOTAKE..Asst. Mgr., Engrg. Dept., Mitsui & Co., 25 Madison Ave.,
                                New York.
339 c THOMAS, MORRIS A.....Operating Engr., Pacific Creosoting Co., Creosote, Wash.
· 87 c TIFFANY, C. W.........Gen. Mgr., Acme Tie Co., Reed City, Mich.
192 c TILLEY, C. M..........Timber Treating Inspector, Southern Ry., Washington, D. C.
197 c TOWNSEND, T. G.......Timber Treating Inspector, Southern Ry., Washington, D. C.
 16 a TOWNSLEY, WM., JR....Grasselli Chemical Co., The Arcade, Cleveland, O.
139 c TRUMBULL, M. K.......Vice-Prest., National Lumber & Creosoting Co., 1209 Com-
                                merce Bldg., Kansas City, Mo.

109 a UNDERWOOD, F. D......Prest., Erie Railroad, Hudson Terminal, New York.

 17 c VALENTINE, H. S.......Supt., Eppinger & Russell Co., Jacksonville, Fla.
 65 c VAN METRE, RICKER...Joyce-Watkins Co., 332 S. Michigan Ave., Chicago, Ill.
207 a von BERNUTH, OSCAR...Prest., Lembcke, von Bernuth Co., 171 Madison Ave., New
                                York.
141 c von LEER, H. J.........Treating Inspector, Baltimore & Ohio R. R. Co., Madison, Ill.
 46 c von SCHRENK, DR. H....Consulting Engineer, Tower Grove & Fladd Aves., St. Louis,
                                Mo.

326 c WADDELL, KENNETH M.Chemist, Santa Fe Tie & Lumber Preserving Co.,
                                Albuquerque, N. M.
256 c WALLACE, H...........Supt., Canada Creosoting Co., Ltd., Trenton, Ontario, Can.
111 a WALSH, P. R...........Prest., Walsh-Griffith Tie & Timber Co., 718 Title Guaranty
                                Bldg., St. Louis, Mo.
 81 c WATERMAN, J. H.......Supt. of Timber Preservation, C., B. & Q. R. R. Co., Gales-
                                burg, Ill.
150 c WATKINS, W. T.........Prest., Joyce-Watkins Co., 332 S. Michigan Ave., Chicago, Ill.
134 c WEBER, J. M...........Supt., Ohio Wood Preserving Co., Orrville, O.
173 c WEGENER, RALPH H....Inspector, St. Paul & Tacoma Lumber Co., 902 North M. St.,
                                Tacoma, Wash.

305 a WEGENER, RICHARD....Preservatives Salesman, 627 27th St., Milwaukee, Wis.
 79 h WEISS, HOWARD F.....Director, Forest Products Laboratory, Madison, Wis.
171 c WELSH, C. T.............Asst. Plant Operator, Republic Creosoting Co., Plymouth
                              Bldg., Minneapolis, Minn.
177 c WHITE, THOS............Asst. Mgr., American Creosote Works, Station B, New
                              Orleans, La.
149 c WIGGETT, C. H..........Supt. Tie Plant, El Paso & Southwestern System,
                              Alamogordo, N. M.
 47 c WILLIAMS, J. C........Supt. Wood-Preserving Works, Barber Asphalt Paving Co.,
                              Maurer, N. J.
138 c WILLIAMS, R. R........Vice-Prest. & Treas., Indiana Tie Co., Citizens National Bank
                              Bldg., Evansville, Ind.
245 c WILLIAMSON, H. E.....Gen. Foreman Timber Preserving Plant, C., B. & Q. R. R.,
                              307 E. First St., Sheridan, Wyo.
102 c WINSLOW, CARLILE P..Engineer in Forest Products, Forest Products Laboratory,
                              Madison, Wis.
125 c WINSLOW, GEOFFREY..Mgr., Creosoting Dept., St. Paul & Tacoma Lumber Co.,
                              Tacoma, Wash.
235 c WIRTH, PHILIPP........Prest., Anthrol Wood Preserving Co., 332 Spring St.,
                              New York.
259 c WOODWARD, G. W......Asst. Supt. Timber Preserving Plant, B., R. & P. Ry. Co.,
                              Bradford, Pa.
298 c WRIGHT, W. E.........Manager Sales, Jennison-Wright Co., 313 Huron St.,
                              Toledo, O.

    c ZELLER, W. C...........Supt., American Creosoting Co., Newark, N. J.
234 c ZWINGAUER, N.........Director, Rutger Works, Lutzowstrasse, Berlin, Germany.

Corrected to December 1, 1916.

BIBLIOGRAPHY OF WOOD PRESERVATION.

PUBLICATIONS:

Associated Factory Mutual Fire Insurance Companies, Inspection
Dept., Boston, 1915.
> *Dry Rot:* F. J. Hoxie.

McGraw-Hill Book Co., New York. 1915-1916.
> *Preservation of Structural Timber:* H. F. Weiss.

Pettibone, Sawtell & Co., Chicago, 1904.
> *Preservation of Timber:* Samuel M. Rowe.

Southern Pine Association, New Orleans, La., 1916.
> *Floors of Service.*

D. Van Nostrand Publishing Co., New York, 1885.
> *The Preservation of Timber by the Use of Antiseptics:*
> Samuel B. Boulton.

West Coast Lumber Manufacturers' Association and Association of
Creosoting Companies of Pacific Coast, Seattle, Wash., 1916.
> *Creosoted Douglas Fir Paving Blocks.*
>
> *Structural Timber Handbook on Pacific Coast Woods:*
> O. P. M. Goss and Carl Heinmiller.

U. S. Dept. of Agriculture, Forest Service, Washington, D. C.

Bulletin	41.	*Seasoning of Timber*	1903
"	50.	*Cross-Tie Forms and Rail Fastenings with Special Reference to Treated Timbers*	1904
"	51.	*Report of Condition of Treated Timbers Laid in Texas, Feb. 1902*	1904
"	70.	*Effect of Moisture on Strength and Stiffness of Wood*	1906
"	78.	*Wood Preservation in the United States*	1909
"	84.	*Preservative Treatment of Poles*	1911
"	88.	*Properties and Uses of Douglas Fir*	1911
"	95.	*Uses of Commercial Woods of United States: Cedars, Cypresses and Sequoias*	1911
"	99.	*Uses of Commercial Woods of United States: Pines.*	1911
"	107.	*The Preservation of Mine Timbers*	1912
"	108.	*Tests of Structural Timbers*	1912
"	112.	*Fire-Killed Douglas Fir: A Study of Its Rate of Deterioration, Usability, and Strength*	1912
"	118.	*Prolonging the Life of Cross-Ties*	1912
"	126.	*Experiments in the Preservative Treatment of Red Oak and Hard Maple Cross-Ties*	1913
Circular	39.	*Experiments on the Strength of Treated Timber*	1908
"	80.	*The Fractional Distillation of Coal-Tar Creosote*	1907
"	98.	*Quantity and Character of Creosote in Well-Preserved Timbers*	1907
"	101.	*The Open Tank Method for the Treatment of Timber*	1907
"	104.	*Brush and Tank Pole Treatments*	1907

U. S. Dept. of Agriculture, Forest Service—*(Continued)*.

Circular 111.   *Prolonging the Life of Mine Timbers* 1907
  "   112.   *The Analysis and Grading of Creosotes* 1908
  "   117.   *The Preservative Treatment of Fence Posts* ... 1907
  "   128.   *Preservation of Piling Against Marine Wood Borers* 1908
  "   132.   *The Seasoning and Preservative Treatment of Hemlock and Tamarack Cross-Ties* 1908
  "   134.   *The Estimation of Moisture in Creosoted Wood* 1908
  "   136.   *The Seasoning and Preservative Treatment of Arborvitae Poles* 1908
  "   139.   *A Primer of Wood Preservation* 1908
  "   141.   *Wood Paving in the United States* 1908
  "   146.   *Experiments with Railway Cross-Ties* 1908
  "   147.   *Progress in Chestnut Pole Preservation* 1908
  "   151.   *Preservative Treatment of Loblolly Pine Cross-Arms* 1908
  "   164.   *Properties and Uses of Southern Pines* 1909
  "   186.   *Consumption of Wood Preservatives and Quantity of Wood Treated in 1910* 1911
  "   188.   *Volatilization of Various Fractions of Creosote After Their Injection into Wood* 1911
  "   189.   *Strength Values of Structural Timbers* 1912
  "   190.   *A Visual Method of Determining the Penetration of Inorganic Salts in Treated Wood* 1911
  "   191.   *Modification of Sulphonation Test for Creosote* 1911
  "   192.   *Prevention of Sap Stain in Lumber* 1912
  "   194.   *Progress Report on Wood Paving Experiments in Minneapolis* 1912
  "   198.   *Condition of Experimental Chestnut Poles in the Warren-Buffalo and Poughkeepsie-Newton Square Lines After Five and Eight Years' Service* 1912
  "   199.   *Quantity and Quality of Creosote Found in Two Treated Piles After Long Service* 1912
  "   200.   *The Absorption of Creosote by the Cell Walls of Wood* 1912
  "   204.   *Strength Tests of Cross-Arms* 1912
  "   206.   *Commercial Creosotes* 1912
  "   209.   *Service Tests of Ties* 1912

U. S. Department of Agriculture.

Bulletin 12.   *Uses of Commercial Woods of United States: Beech, Birches, and Maples* 1913
  "   67.   *Tests of Rocky Mountain Woods for Telephone Poles* 1914
  "   77.   *Rocky Mountain Mine Timbers* 1914
  "   101.   *Relative Resistance of Various Conifers to Injection with Creosote* 1914
  "   145.   *Tests of Wood Preservatives* 1915

U. S. Dept. of Agriculture—*(Continued)*.
Bulletin 227. *The Toxicity to Fungi of Various Oils and
            Salts* 1915
    "   286. *Strength Tests of Structural Timbers Treated
            by Commercial Wood-Preserving Processes*... 1915
    "   333. *Termites, or "White Ants" in the United
            States: Their Damage, and Methods of Pre-
            vention* 1916

Farmers' Bulletin 387. *The Preservative Treatment of Farm
            Timbers* 1910

Yearbook.   *Fungous Diseases of Forest Trees*........... 1900
Extracts   *Recent Progress in Timber Preservation*...... 1903
            Prolonging Life of Telephone Poles......... 1905

U. S. Dept. of Agriculture, Bureau of Entomology.
Circular 127. *Insect Injuries to the Wood of Dying and
            Dead Trees*................................. 1910
    "   134. *Damage to Telephone and Telegraph Poles by
            Wood-Boring Insects* 1911

U. S. Dept. of Agriculture, Bureau of Plant Industry.
Bulletin 14. *The Decay of Timber and Methods of Pre-
            venting it* 1902
    "   114. *Sap-Rot and other Diseases of Red Gum*...... 1907

U. S. Army, Engineer Bureau.

Professional Memoirs. *Creosotes and Creosoting:*
            Capt. John C. Oakes...............April-June, 1909

U. S. Dept. of State.
Daily Consular and Trade Reports:
            Processes for Fireproofing Wood......Jan. 23, 1914

U. S. Dept. of the Interior, Bureau of Mines, Washington, D. C.
Bulletin.   *Coal-Tar Products:* H. C. Porter........... 1915

U. S. Treasury Dept., Public Health and Marine Hospital Service,
    Hygiene Laboratory, Washington, D. C.
Bulletin 22. *Chloride of Zinc as a Deodorant, Antiseptic,
            and Germicide* 1905

Smithsonian Institution, Washington, D. C.
            Report on Preservation of Wood.............1864

Iowa Agricultural Experiment Station, Ames, Iowa.
Bulletin 158. *Preservative Treatment of Fence Posts:*
            G. B. MacDonald......................... 1916

Maryland State Board of Forestry, Baltimore, Md.
            Increasing the Durability of Fence Posts:
            F. W. Beasley.............................. 1912

Missouri Agricultural Experiment Station, Columbus, Mo.
Circular 51. *How to Prolong the Life of Fence Posts:*
            T. A. Ferguson............................. 1911

PROCEEDINGS:

American Association for the Advancement of Science.

Paraffin Bodies in Coal-Tar Creosote and Their Bearing on Specifications: S. R. Church and John Morris Weiss.................................. 1914

Creosoted Wood Block: Geo. W. Tillson............ 1915

American Electric Railway Engineering Association.

Some Factors Affecting the Application of Wood Preservatives to Electric Railways: C. P. Winslow and C. H. Teesdale.............. 1915

American Iron and Steel Institute, New York.

Byproducts Recovered in the Manufacture of Coke: W. H. Childs...........................May 26, 1916

American Institute of Electrical Engineers, New York.

Recent Results Obtained from the Preservative Treatment of Telephone Poles: F. L. Rhodes and R. F. Hosford..................................... 1915

American Railway Bridge & Building Association, Elgin, Ill.

*Report of Committee on Wood Preservation....*1908-1912
Preservation of Timber............................. 1913
Annual Cost of Treated and Untreated Piles in Trestles 1914

American Railway Engineering Association, Chicago, Ill.

Changes Which Take Place in Coal-Tar Creooste During Exposure: Hermann von Schrenk, E. B. Fulks and A. L. Kammerer..... 1907

*Report of Committee on Wood Preservation.....*1909-1916

Precautions to be Observed in Burnettizing Ties: Octave Chanute.................................... 1909

The Microscopical Structure and Physical Condition of Wood as Affects Penetration by Preservatives: Harry D. Tiemann......................... 1909

Condition of Treated Timbers Laid in Texas in 1902: Carlile P. Winslow........................... 1910

Tentative Grouping of Ties for Experimental Preservative Treatment: Howard F. Weiss......... 1910

Fungi Which Live on Structural Timber: C. J. Humphrey 1910

Fourth Progress Report on Tests on Treated Ties: W. K. Hatt................................... 1910

Note on the Strength of Ties Treated with Crude Oil: W. K. Hatt............................... 1911

The Electrical Resistance of Timber as Affected by Treatment with Preservatives: J. T. Butterfield 1911

Grouping of Timbers for Antiseptic Treatment...... 1912

Air Seasoning of Ties: Wm. H. Kemper......1913-1914

The Use of Refined Coal-Tar in the Creosoting Industry: Dr. Hermann von Schrenk and Alfred L. Kammerer 1914

Effect of Creosoting on Strength of Oregon Fir Piling: H. B. MacFarland....................... 1914

American Wood-Preservers' Association—*(Continued)*.

Classification of the Proper Condition of Timber for Treatment: A. S. Case.................... 1906

General Conditions Governing Wood-Preserving Plants: D. Burkhalter..................... 1906

The Future Progress of Wood Preservation: Carl G. Crawford..................... 1906

A Sketch of Methods and Practice in Use at Mexican Central Railway Company's Plant at Aguascalientes: J. E. Philippi..................... 1906

Progress of Timber Preservation in 1906: Carl G. Crawford..................... 1907

The Advantages and Disadvantages of Steaming: O. Chanute..................... 1907

The Causes of Decay in Timber: C. W. Berry...... 1907

History of Wood Preservation in America: Octavo Chanute..................... 1909

Heartwoods Which can be Treated: H. J. Valentine. 1909

The Treatment of Dead Timbers: C. W. Berry...... 1909

The Proper Grouping of Timbers for Treating: J. S. Baker..................... 1909

Inflammability of Treated Timbers: H. M. Rollins... 1909

Quantity and Quality of Creosote for Treating Piling: R. J. Calder..................... 1909

Use of Crude Oil as a Timber Preservative, and the Best Method of Application: George E. Rex.... 1909

Should an Attempt be made to Air-Season Timber Before Treating in the Southern Part of the United States: R. L. Allardyce..................... 1909

What is the Best Power for Moving Ties and Material Throughout the Yard and Into the Retorts: J. B. Card..................... 1909

Treating in Open-Tanks..................... 1909

Experience in Injury to Men from Handling Creosoted Material..................... 1909

Effect of Timbers Treated With Creosote or Zinc Chloride on Electric Currents Passing Through Other Materials in Contact With the Timber..... 1909

Creosoting Douglas Fir: David Allerton........... 1909

What Effect Does the Time of Cutting Timber Have on the Rate of Seasoning and Treatment of Same: J. C. Williams..................... 1910

Economics of Cables, Electricity or Locomotives in Moving Materials at Plants: Andrew Gibson... 1910

Inflammability of Treated Timber: H. M. Rollins... 1910

Advantages and Economy of Various Retort Doors: David Allerton..................... 1910

Advantages and Economy of Various Retort Doors: S. M. Rowe..................... 1910

Precaution to be Observed for Prevention of Fire in Creosoting Plants: Lowry Smith..................... 1910

American Wood-Preservers' Association—*(Continued)*.

*General Review of Timber Treating in this Country,
with Special Reference to Causes That Have Been
and are Retarding its More Universal Adoption:*
John T. Logan..................................... 1911

Review of Development in Timber-Treating Industry:
Walter Buehler 1911

*Benefits Derived from Attending Annual Meetings of
the Wood-Preservers' Association by Members
of the Association:* Wm. Townsley, Jr......... 1911

*What Percentage of Creosote Oil can be withdrawn
from Wood by Subsequent Vacuum:*
C. D. Chanute..................................... 1911

*Asphaltic Oils as Applied to the Preservation of
Railroad Ties:* Frank W. Cherrington.......... 1911

Impurities in Zinc Chloride: C. Marshall Taylor.... 1911

The Production of the Wooden Cross Tie:
A. R. Joyce..................................... 1912

Economic Material for Boat and Barge Construction:
A. E. Hageboeck................................. 1912

Cutting and Seasoning of Timber: A. Meyer....... 1912

Scientific Management of Timber-Preserving Plants:
D. Burkhalter................................... 1912

Efficiency in Plant Operation: E. A. Sterling....... 1912

Creosote Oil Specifications and Methods of Analysis:
S. R. Church................................... 1912

Evaporation of Creosote and Crude Oils:
P. E. Fredendoll................................. 1912

*Comparison of the Absorption and Expansion of
Properties of Wood Paving Blocks when Treated
with Paving Oil of a Specific Gravity of 1.2 and
Creosote Oil of Specific Gravity of 1.055:*
H. M. Rollins................................... 1912

*Wood Block Pavement from a Construction Stand-
point:* Day I. Okes............................. 1912

Creosoted Wood Paving Blocks: A. E. Larkin...... 1912

*Structure of Commercial Woods in Relation to the
Injection of Preservatives:* Howard F. Weiss... 1912

Creosotes and Creosoting Oil: David Allerton....... 1912

Creosote Specifications and Analysis:
Dr. Hermann von Schrenk...................... 1912

*Arrangement of Yard; Piling Ties and Timber and
Kindred Subjects:* J. H. Waterman............. 1912

Treating Seasoned vs. Unseasoned Ties:
F. J. Angier................................... 1912

*Inspectors and Inspection of Material and Treatments
at Commercial Plants:* R. L. Allardyce........ 1912

Preservation of Power Transmission Poles:
W. R. Wheaton................................. 1912

The Production and Supply of Coal-Tar Creosote:
E. A. Sterling................................. 1913

*A Comparison of Zinc Chloride with Coal-Tar Creo-
sote for Preserving Cross Ties:* H. F. Weiss... 1913

American Wood-Preservers' Association—(Continued).

Details of Methods of Testing Creosote Oil........ 1914

Creosote Oil: P. C. Reilly........................ 1914

The Use of Refined Coal-Tar in the Creosoting Industry: Dr. Hermann von Schrenk and Alfred L. Kammerer.................................. 1914

Preliminary Work in Fireproofing Wood: Robert E. Prince.............................. 1914

A Comparison of Wood Paving in European Countries and the United States: S. R. Church............ 1914

Report of Creosoted Piling in Galveston Bay Bridge of Santa Fe Railway........................... 1914

The Construction of Creosoted Wood Block Pavements: R. S. Manley.......................... 1914

Creosoted Wood Block Pavements: Harry G. Davis. 1914

Results Obtained by Piling Creosoted Wood Blocks Closely in Cages and the Saving Effected Thereby: R. H. White................................. 1914

New Type of Paving Block Plant: J. B. Card....... 1914

The Preservation of Wood by Means of Corrosive Sublimate (Kyanizing): Dr. Friedrich Moll..... 1914

The Protection of Ties from Mechanical Destruction: Howard F. Weiss........................... 1914

Future Tie Material in the United States: H. H. Gibson................................. 1914

Treatment of Piling and Timber According to Condition of Use and Exposure: E. L. Powell........ 1914

Some Facts which I have gathered from Observation and Inspection of Experimental Ties: J. H. Waterman............................... 1914

Steaming Process for Ties and Timbers............. 1914

Air Pumps vs. Hydraulic Pumps for Injecting Preservatives into Wood: F. J. Angier............ 1914

The Effect of Varying the Preliminary Air Pressure in Treating Ties upon the Absorption and Penetration of Creosote: Clyde H. Teesdale......... 1914

Mechanical Handling of Railroad Cross Ties and Timbers at Timber Preservation Plants: Lambert T. Ericson............................ 1914

Discussion of Preceding Paper: F. J. Angier, J. H. Waterman, William A. Fisher, Amos Smith and Carl G. Crawford......................... 1914

Tram Cars and their Construction: J. H. Grow...... 1914

Methods of Keeping Tie Records: E. T. Howson.... 1914

The Yale Forest School: Samuel J. Record......... 1914

Address of George S. Wood, of the Forest Products Exposition 1914

Quantity of Wood Preservatives Consumed and Amount of Wood Treated in the United States in 1913: Clark W. Gould...................... 1914

Timber-Treating Plants in North America: W. F. Goltra.................................. 1914

American Wood-Preservers' Association—*(Concluded)*.

Laboratory Analysis after Treatment versus Actual Record during Treatment of Creosoted Wood Paving Blocks: Frank W. Cherrington......... 1915

Discussion on Report on Wood Block Paving: E. R. Dutton.................................... 1915

The Bleeding and Swelling of Paving Blocks: Clyde H. Teesdale............................. 1915

Discussion on Bleeding and Swelling of Wood Block Pavements: L. E. Hess and E. R. Dutton....... 1915

Progress in Timber-Treating Industry: J. W. Kendrick................................ 1916

Creosoted Piling and Poles: Frank W. Cherrington.. 1916

Methods of Creosoting Douglas Fir Timbers: O. P. M. Goss................................. 1916

Vacuum Process in Creosoting: John D. Isaacs..... 1916

Notes on Measuring Devices and on Methods of Determining Cubical Contents Per Charge: C. W. Lane.................................. 1916

Selecting and Buying Fuel: W. H. Grady........... 1916

The Foreign Creosote Oil Situation: G. A. Lembcke. 1916

Woods Suitable for Cross Ties: R. Van Metre...... 1916

Quantity of Zinc Chloride Per Tie or Per Cubic Foot of Timber, and Method of Determining the True Strength of the Solution: W. F. Goltra.......... 1916

Marine Borers from the Wood-Preservers' Standpoint: Dr. L. F. Shackell...................... 1916

Preservative Specifications for Wood Paving Blocks: A. E. Larkin.................................. 1916

Fungi Which Grow on Untreated Ties or Untreated Wood: Dr. H. von Schrenk.................... 1916

Treated Wood Block for Factory Flooring and Miscellaneous Uses: C. H. Teesdale................ 1916

Service Tests of Wood Block Paving............... 1916

Woods Suitable for Cross Ties: Carlile P. Winslow and John A. Newlin........ 1916

Conservation of our Natural Resources: F. H. Newell 1916

Service Tests of Cross Ties......................... 1916

Durability Records of Cross Ties: Carlile P. Winslow and C. H. Teesdale.......... 1916

Service Tests of Bridge and Structural Timber....... 1916

Revision of the Constitution: John Foley.......... 1916

Quantity of Wood Preservatives Consumed and Amount of Wood Treated by Wood-Preserving Plants in the U. S. in 1915: R. K. Helphenstine.. 1916

U. S. Patents on Wood Preservation: D. D. Berolzheimer............................ 1916

Bibliography of Wood-Boring Crustaceans: Dr. F. Moll.................................. 1916

Arkansas Good Roads and Drainage Association, Little Rock, Ark.

Creosoted Wood Block Paving: Walter Buehler.... 1916

Association of Engineering Societies, St. Louis, Mo.
> *The Preservation of Railway Ties and Timber by the Use of Antiseptics:* Joseph P. Card......April, 1887
>
> *Wood-Preserving and Uses of Treated Lumber:* F. A. Weaver....................May, 1914
>
> *Timber Conservation and Preservation in the United States:* E. L. Powell.....................May, 1914
>
> *Preservative Treatment of Timber:* J. M. Goldman ....Oct., 1914
>
> *The Creosoting of Cross-Ties as Practiced by American Railroads:* O. C. Steinmayer.........Mar., 1915

Engineering Society of Western Pennsylvania.
> *The Preservation of Structural Timbers from Decay:* C. P. Winslow.................................. 1910

Engineers' Club of Philadelphia, Pa.
> *Methods and Economic Aspects of Modern Timber Preservation:* Gellert Alleman.................. 1907

International Congress of Applied Chemistry.
> *Tests to Determine the Commercial Value of Wood Preservatives:* H. F. Weiss. Vol. 13, Section 6a 1912
>
> *Antiseptic Tests of Wood-Preserving Oils:* A. L. Dean and C. R. Downs. Vol. 13, Section 6a...... 1912

International Engineering Congress, San Francisco, Cal.
> *Preservative Treatment of Timber:* H. F. Weiss and C. H. Teesdale........................... 1915

Louisiana Engineering Society, New Orleans, La.
> *Creosoted Wood Block Pavements:* F. P. Hamilton ....August, 1916

National Electric Light Association, New York.
> *Report of Committee on Preservative Treatment of Poles and Cross-Arms......*May, 1910 and May, 1911
>
> *Poles and Pole Preservation:* Russell A. Griffin.... 1913

National Fire Protective Association.
> *Tests on the Inflammability of Untreated Wood and of Wood Treated with Fire-Retarding Compounds:* R. E. Prince......................... 1915

National Lumber Manufacturers' Association, Chicago, Ill.
> *Preservative Treatment of Farm Timbers:* E. A. Sterling................................. 1916

New England Railroad Club, Boston, Mass.
> *A General Consideration of Timber Under Conditions of Modern Demand and Growth:* Hermann von Schrenk 1907

New York Railroad Club.
> *The Seasoning and Preservative Treatment of Wooden Cross-Ties:* F. J. Angier.................... 1910

Railway Storekeepers' Association, Cleveland, O.
> *Treatment of Lumber and the Handling of Same Before and After Treatment:* Hermann von Schrenk 1909

St. Louis (Mo.) Railway Club.
> *Recent Progress in Testing Wood Used by the Railroads:* H. F. Weiss........................... 1916

Western Society of Engineers, Chicago, Ill.
  Preservative Treatment of Timber: O. Chanute.April, 1900
  Preservation of Timber: S. M. Rowe.........June, 1900
  Factors Which Cause the Decay of Wood: Hermann
    von Schrenk...............................May, 1901
  Timber Treating Plants: W. W. Curtis..........Oct.,1903
  Wood Preservation from an Engineering Standpoint:
    C. T. Barnum.............................June, 1910
Yellow Pine Manufacturers' Association. (Southern Pine Asso-
  ciation.)
  Prevention of Decay in Factory Timbers: F. J.
    Hoxie 1914

PERIODICALS:

American City, New York.
  Wood Block Pavements: H. S. Loud........March, 1916
American Lumberman, Chicago, Ill.
  *Wood Block for Factory Floors.............Nov. 28, 1914
  Impregnation of Timber to Protect it from Fire:
    Dr. F. Moll............................Dec. 26, 1914
  The Preservative Treatment of Wooden Silos: G. M.
    Hunt ....March 13, 1915
  Preservative Treatment of Wood:
    E. W. Peters............................Apr. 17, 1915
  Wood Preservation: H. E. Horrocks........July 17, 1915
  *Rot in Stored Lumber; A Danger to Builders and
    Dealers:* C. J. Humphrey..............Aug. 14, 1915
  *How Strengths of Woods are Tested........Aug. 7, 1915
  *Silo Preservatives that are Safe............Sept. 11, 1915
  *Demand for Creosoted Wood Conduits......Oct. 2, 1915
  *Wood Blocks Treated Economically........Nov. 20, 1915
  *Fire Tests of Wood at the Forest Products Labora-
    tory:* Clyde H. Teesdale................Dec. 11, 1915
  *Test Proves Wood's Fire-Resistive Qualities..Dec. 18, 1915
American Roofer.
  Fire-Proofing Wooden Shingles: H. F. Weiss..Dec., 1914
Armour Engineer, Chicago, Ill.
  The Preservation of Wood from Decay: Clyde H.
    Teesdale ....March, 1915
Canadian Engineer, Toronto, Ontario.
  *Battle Against Rot...........................Nov. 19, 1914
  Creosoted Wood Block Paving:
    Andrew F. Macallum...................April 15, 1915
  Creosoted Wood Block Pavements:
    Andrew F. Macallum...................Mar. 30, 1916
Electric Railway Journal, New York. -
  Wood Preservation: A. L. Kuehn............Dec. 3, 1910
  *Economical Use of Wood and Preservation of
    Timber:* E. W. Bright.................Dec. 19, 1914

Electric Traction Weekly, Cleveland, O.
>   *Timber Preservation:* Carlile P. Winslow.......... 1911

Engineering News, New York.
>   *Creosoting Plant of the Pacific Creosoting Co., Eagle Harbor, Wash*...........................Nov. 3, 1910
>   *Marine Wood Destroyers in the Waters of the South Atlantic Ports:* W. H. Faucette..........Jan. 5, 1911
>   *Tie Treating Plant, Louisville & Nashville R. R.*....................................Sept. 24, 1914
>   *New Tie Treating Plant on the Chicago & Northwestern Railway:* L. J. Putman........April 20, 1916
>   *Resin in Yellow Pine for Decay Resistance:* F. J. Hoxie and Dr. Hermann von Schrenk...April 20, 1916

Engineering Record, New York.
>   *Plant of the National Lumber & Creosoting Co.:* Grant B. Shipley.......................July 29, 1911
>   *Factors Affecting Structural Timbers:* H. S. Betts.............................Aug. 29, 1914
>   *Efficiency of Various Parts of Coal-Tar Creosote Against Marine Borers:* C. H. Teesdale.Sept. 12, 1914
>   *How the Wood-Preserving Industry can Avoid Possible Injury Resulting from the War:* C. H. Teesdale ....Sept. 26, 1914
>   *Decay in Wooden Bleachers:* C. H. Teesdale..Oct. 3, 1914
>   *Creosoted Wood Blocks Suitable for Bridge Floors if Fire-Proofed:* L. T. Ericson..........June 5, 1915

Forestry Quarterly, Toronto Canada.
>   *Preservative Treatment of Wood:* Irving W. Bailey........................March, 1913
>   *Preservation of Mine Timbers:* Dr. F. Moll..Vol. 13, 1915

Journal of Industrial & Engineering Chemistry, Easton, Pa.
>   *Method of Determining the Amount of Zinc Chloride in Treated Wood:* Ernest Bateman.......Jan., 1914
>   *Toxicity of Various Wood Preservatives:* C J. Humphrey and Ruth M. Fleming.. . {Feb., 1914 {Aug., 1915
>   *The Application of the Davis Spot Test in the Preliminary Examination of Creosotes:* H. C. Cloukey...........................Nov., 1915
>   *Study of the Composition of Water-Gas-Tar:* C. R. Downs and A. L. Dean..............May, 1914
>   *New Method for Determining Zinc in Treated Wood:* M. Hume Bedford and R. Pfansteil........Oct., 1914
>   *Specific Gravity; Its Determination for Tars, Oils and Pitches:* John Morris Weiss..............Jan., 1915

Lumber Trade Journal, New Orleans, La.
>   *Preservation of Timber by Use of Fluoric Salts:* Dr. F. Moll............................Jan. 15, 1915
>   *Measuring Moisture in Green or Dry Lumber:* S. D. Curtis...........................April 1, 1915

Lumber World Review, Chicago, Ill.
>   *Domestic Supply of Wood Preservatives:*
>   Clyde H. Teesdale......................Oct. 19, 1914
>   *Modern Uses of Wood:*
>   Dr. Hermann von Schrenk..............April 25, 1915

Mining & Engineering World, Chicago, Ill.
>   *Seasoning and Preservative Treatment of Mine*
>   *Timbers* ....May 18, 1912

Municipal Engineering, Chicago, Ill.
>   *Asphaltic Oils, Economical Wood Preservatives:*
>   Frank W. Cherrington.....................May, 1911
>   *Durability of Creosoted Block Pavements Increased*
>   *by Modern Methods of Treatment:*
>   Frank W. Cherrington....................Dec., 1915
>   *Wood·Blocks for Street Paving: Their Treatment*
>   *and Handling* ....May, 1916

Municipal Journal, New York.
>   *Experiments with Wood Paving Blocks:*
>   Clyde H. Teesdale......................May 6, 1915

Railway Age Gazette, New York.
>   *Effect of the War on Timber Preservation*..April 13, 1915
>   *Creosoted Wood Block Floors for Railroad*
>   *Buildings* ....Dec. 17, 1915

Railway & Engineering Review, Chicago, Ill.
>   *Chemical Treatment of Timber:*
>   Hermann von Schrenk..................June 6, 1903
>   *Preservation of Timber from Decay:*
>   W. F. Goltra............................Oct. 7, 1911
>   *Steaming Timber Before Treating with Preservatives:*
>   O. Chanute ....Mar. 2, 1913

Railway Maintenance Engineer, Chicago, Ill.
>   *Penetration of Preservatives:* Lowry Smith....June, 1916

Railway Review, Chicago, Ill.
>   *Air Seasoning of Timber:* .W. H. Kempfer..Jan. 10, 1914
>   *Tie Timber and the Unnecessary Wear and Tear of*
>   *Track:* Geo. E. Rex....................Sept. 18, 1915
>   *Proper Oil for Creosoting Wood Blocks for Paving:*
>   P. C. Reilly............................Jan. 22, 1916

Scientific American Supplement, New York.
>   *The Modern Electrical Process for Rapidly Drying*
>   *and Preserving Wood*....................Oct. 31, 1914
>   *Marine Wood Borers:* Clyde H. Teesdale....Dec. 5, 1914

Southern Lumberman, Nashville, Tenn.
>   *Impregnation of Preservatives:*
>   Samuel J. Record......................Dec. 19, 1914
>   *Variation in Weight and Strength of Timber:*
>   J. A. Newlin............................Jan. 22, 1916
>   *Sanitary Handling of Timber:*
>   C. J. Humphrey........................April 1, 1916

Telephony, Chicago.

Study of the Use and Preservation of Wooden Poles:
Dr. F. Moll..........................April 11-25, 1914

Service Tests of Treated and Untreated Telephone Poles: Clyde H. Teesdale...............April 3, 1915

Treatment of Poles and Cross-Arms with Preservatives:
J. B. Wilkinson.........................April 27, 1915

University of Washington Forest Club Annual, Seattle, Wash.

The Value of Ammonium Polysulphide as a Wood Preservative: Donald H. Clark........Vol. III, 1915

West Coast Lumberman, Seattle, Wash.

Dry Rot in Buildings of Mill Construction:
Howard B. Oakleaf......................Dec. 15, 1915

Preservative Treatments: Geo. E. Rex........Jan. 1, 1916

Wood-Preservers' Bulletin, (Wood-Preserving), Baltimore, Md.

Penetration of Timber by Preservatives:
Clyde H. Teesdale..................Vol. I No. 3, 1914

Specific Gravity and Weight of Some Important American Woods ....Vol. I No. 3, 1914

Toxicity Tests on Wood Preservatives:
Carlile P. Winslow................Vol. I No. 3, 1914

St. Helens Creosoting Plant, St. Helens, Oregon ....Vol. I No. 3, 1914

Wood-Preserving, Baltimore, Md.

Baltimore & Ohio Timber Preserving Plant, Green Spring, W. Va..............Vol. II No. 1, 1915

The Galesburg (Ill.) Tie Plant of the Chicago, Burlington & Quincy Railroad.....Vol. II No. 2, 1915

Development of Demand for Wood Blocks:
R. S. Manley......................Vol. II No. 2, 1915

The Port Reading Creosoting Plant of the Philadelphia & Reading and Central R. R. of New Jersey..................Vol. II No. 3, 1915

Prolonging the Life of Poles:
W. F. Goltra............Vol. II No. 3 & No. 4, 1915
Vol. III No. 1, 1916

Zinc Chloride as a Preservative:
Alfred H. Clarke.................Vol. II No. 4, 1915

The Preservative Treatment of Farm Timbers:
Geo. M. Hunt.....................Vol. II No. 4, 1915

Saving Creosote Oil in the Treatment of Piling:
Clyde H. Teesdale................Vol. II No. 4, 1915

The Central of Georgia Treating Plant..Vol. II No. 4, 1915

The Economic Use of Cross-Ties on the Baltimore & Ohio R. R.........Vol. III No. 2, 1916

An Experimental Wood-Preserving Laboratory:
W. G. Mitchell...................Vol. III No. 2, 1916

Decay: An Important Factor in Plant Management:
Geo. M. Hunt.....................Vol. III No. 2, 1916

Treating Ties for the Grand Rapids & Ind., the Pere Marquette and Pennsylvania Lines West ....Vol. III No. 2, 1916

Wood-Preserving—*(Concluded)*.

A Pacific Coast Timber-Treating Plant
    (Pacific Creosoting Co., Seattle, Wash.):
    H. E. Horrocks..................Vol. III No. 3, 1916

The Relation Between the Specific Gravity of
    Zinc Chloride Solutions and Their Con-
    centrations: E. Bateman........Vol. III No. 3, 1916

Experiments in Treating Ties in India:
    Ralph S. Pearson.............Vol. III No. 3 & 4, 1916

Wood-Preserving Plants in the Vicinity of New
    York ....Vol. III No. 4, 1916

Wood-Preserving Plant at Newark, N. J.:
    E. G. Draper...................Vol. III No. 4, 1916

Wood-Preserving Plant at Maurer, N. J.:
    John C. Williams...............Vol. III No. 4, 1916

Use of Fluorides in Wood Preservation:
    C. H. Teesdale..................Vol. III No. 4, 1916

*Treated Wood in New York Bridges.*Vol. III No. 4, 1916

Relation Between Toxicity and Volatility of
    Creosote Oils—I: E. Bateman..Vol. III. No. 4, 1916

*Treatment of White-Oak Ties....*Vol. III No. 3 & 4, 1916

An Experiment in the Preservative Treatment of
    Fence Posts—I:
    Morris Greenberg...............Vol. III No. 4, 1916

www.ingramcontent.com/pod-product-compliance
Lightning Source LLC
Chambersburg PA
CBHW081235280526
45787CB00006B/2668